Party Central

A MONTH-BY-MONTH GUIDE TO ENTERTAINING ON THE CHEAP

Festive and Frugal Ideas
for Every Occasion

A PERIGEE BOOK

A Perigee Book
Published by The Berkley Publishing Group
A division of Penguin Group (USA) Inc.
375 Hudson Street
New York, New York 10014

Book design by Don Morris Design
Cover design by Don Morris Design, Toby Fox, and Ben Gibson

Edited by Kathleen Hackett

The photograph credits that appear on page 189 are
incorporated herein by reference.

Perigee trade paperback edition: October 2004

Visit our website at www.penguin.com.

This book has been cataloged by the Library of Congress.

Printed in the United States of America
10   9   8   7   6   5   4   3   2   1

Budget Living Magazine
317 Madison Avenue, Suite 2300
New York, New York 10017
212-687-6060; fax: 212-687-5222

Budget Living magazine is published bimonthly. Subscription prices,
payable in U.S. funds, are $19.95 for one year (six issues). Additional postage:
In Canada, add $10, and in all other foreign countries, add $15 per year.
To subscribe or renew: Call 800-588-1644 or visit www.BudgetLivingMedia.com.

Budget Living, *Spend Smart. Live Rich.*, *Home Cheap Home*, and *Party Central*
are trademarks of Budget Living LLC.

Acknowledgments

IF THERE'S ONE THING WE KNOW HERE AT *BUDGET LIVING*, it's how to have a good time. Sure, our tiny, tireless staff toils around the clock, but when that clock strikes, say, 7 P.M., you'll likely find us breaking open the Budweiser, cranking up the stereo, and digging into delivery pizza. Champagne and caviar it's not, but we've never believed that fancy food makes the fete. Rather, a great party has everything to do with assembling a great guest list. It's the mix of people, not the money spent, that matters. And we've gathered one hell of a gifted group to work on *Party Central*. Just about every member of the *BL* staff came to the table, namely Alex Bhattacharji, Danielle Dowling, Laura Fenton, Gregory Garry, Sheri Geller, Sarah Humphreys, Winnie Lee, Lynne Palazzi, Rose Reis, John Voelcker, Caroline Whitbeck, and Alexa Yablonski. Kathleen Hackett, editor of our previous book, *Home Cheap Home*, also took the helm on this one. Don Morris oversaw the design, working with Josh Klenert and Jessica Kasper. And Catherine Whalen, a *Le Cordon Bleu* grad as well as my best childhood friend, developed and edited recipes (in addition to writing two chapters). Checking the facts were Rebecca Geiger, Wendy Giman, Adam Silberberg, and Jan Weed; our copy editing team comprised Steve Selberg, Todd Hodgson, and Kathryn Papacosma; Elizabeth Parson compiled the index.

Most of the following chapters have been adapted from stories that were first published in *Budget Living*. The writers behind those magazine features also deserve credit here. They are Laura Chamorro (July), Laura Fenton (February), Gregory Garry (June), Kathleen Hackett (September), Joann Milivojevic (April), Lynne Palazzi (May), Emma Sussman Starr (March), Courtney Taylor (December), Amy Wilensky (January), Catherine Whalen (October, November), and Caroline Whitbeck (August). Other writers, editors, and producers whose work appears herein include Alison Alfandre, Lansdale Franklin, Julie Mihaly, Joanna Milter, Patricia Thomson, and Allison Tick. The photographers are listed on page 189. Of course, it's the hosts who get any party started, and the following folks invited us to share in their entertaining expertise: Demi Adeniran, Alexandra and Eliot Angle, Jon Carloftis, Nita and Clay Cook, Gabrielle Hamilton, Ebony Snow Hurr and Joe Brody, Elizabeth and William Joyce, Sue and Adam Keller, Melissa Locker and Brian Benavidez, Eric Macaire, Jessica Murnane and Dan Jividen, Felice Pappas and Bill Kearney, Peggy Pierrepont, Courtney Taylor, and Kristen Thiele and Frank Casale.

As always, we'd be lost without Janet Mannheimer and Ellen Marin of Publishing Experts. Thanks also go to Spectragraphic's Michael Breen and Perigee/Penguin's Michelle Howry and John Duff. Finally, a toast to *Budget Living* founders Don Welsh and Eric Rayman: Our little get-together has swelled to proportions I didn't dare anticipate. Yes, it's driven me to drink the occasional cocktail, but Lord knows, it's never ceased to be entertaining.

—SARAH GRAY MILLER, Editor-in-Chief, *Budget Living*

Introd

action

BUDGET LIVING
SPEND SMART · LIVE RICH.

BE SAFE · KEEP COVER CLOSED

www.budgetlivingmedi...

ProCon Marketing

Because You Don't Have Money to Burn

anna get the party started right?
Start right here.
ve got a calendar full of frugal fetes
chat are sure to strike your fancy.

Introduction

If someone asked you to recall the best party you'd ever been to, which one would come to mind? Chances are, it's not that formal wedding with the catered sit-down dinner and choreographed servers dashing hither and thither. Nor is your mother-in-law's stuffy cocktail soiree—loaded with guests as stiff as the scotch and sodas you downed—likely to make the cut either. No, we're willing to bet a year's worth of bash cash that you'd give top honors to the neighbor who, during last year's blizzard, cooked a pot of chili, chilled some beer in the snow, and broke out the Scrabble.

Why is it that the memory of hearty, humble grub and cold brews stays with us far longer than, say, a twirled-up tray of canapés? Just ask any of the folks

Not-So-Trivial Pursuits

You don't have to spend big money to make a big impression. Even the tiniest, cheapest details can set a festive tone. Case in point: These colorful plastic primates, which cost less than a dollar a dozen (www.stuff-o-rama.com) and are more fun than—you guessed it—a barrel of monkeys. Dangling from the rim of a glass, they're guaranteed to enliven your libations.

There's no need to bend over backward to throw a great bash. When you, the host, are relaxed, guests feel comfortable enough to kick off their shoes (or shoe) and boogie to the beat.

It's possible to celebrate holiday traditions without being too traditional. Next Christmas, skip the pine boughs and fir trees and deck your halls with cards (glued to a metal wreath form) and ornaments liberated from their limbs.

behind the parties featured in the chapters herein and they'll give you the same answer: Too much fussin' around ain't fun for anyone, especially the person at the helm. A harried host is a killjoy, no matter how tasty the food, thirst-slaking the drinks, or dashing the decor. So lead by example and relax—a good time for all will surely follow.

Keep in mind that the minute you open the door, partygoers will get a glimpse of the kind of gig they're in for and a clue as to whether they should hold back or cut loose. Answer the bell in bare feet and you'll convey a comfort level that a pair of stilettos never could.

Thankfully, it's easy to keep your cool when your to-do list isn't a mile long. Just serve the kind of food people really love instead of those *amuse-bouches* everybody's afraid to eat. (Ever notice how the deviled eggs—and bottles of Bud—disappear first?) And while clever details certainly make a difference, you don't have to go into debt decorating your digs. Creatively dispatch whatever's on hand and hit the five-and-dime for the rest. Finally, be sure to get your guests into the act. If there's one foolproof way to break an unsettling silence, it's by putting a chopping knife or a martini shaker in the shy guy's hand.

Setting the Stage

Keeping it casual is key, but that's no excuse for sloppy prep work. First impressions say a lot, and attention to detail speaks volumes. So hang on to a little old-fashioned formality; it can go a long way. (Mail your invites or pick up the phone—no E-vites, please; offer your guests drinks the moment they

💡 Plex Appeal

High-maintenance linens aren't the only way to dress a dining table in style. Splurge on a custom-cut sheet of Plexiglass (a six-by-three-foot piece runs $75; see PLASTICS in the Yellow Pages) and you'll get a stain-resistant topper that can showcase—and protect—revolving exhibits of seasonal ephemera.

💡 Old Object, New Trick

Expanding your decor options is easy when you see everyday items in a fresh light. You may not own hurricane lamps, but you probably do have plenty of glass pitchers. So use them to protect candles in the wind.

💡 **Chill Out**

If standard-issue ice buckets leave you cold, think outside the bin—and look around your house for cool alternatives. An enameled pail (above), a gilded wastebasket (below), and a plain metal paint-mixing bucket (bottom) are all capable of serving up cubes.

arrive.) But skip the Waterford highball glasses. Ditto the Wedgwood china. Nowadays, it's okay to set the table with mismatched flea-market finds or even plastic plates, as long as they're well designed.

Clearly, some entertaining traditions should be respected, others rejected—or at least tweaked to suit your personality. At first, the idea of a theme party may seem a tad quaint and restrictive, but believe us: Having a blueprint in place is easier than starting from scratch. Whether it's a holiday like Halloween, an event such as the Kentucky Derby, or something as simple as poker or movie night, all the elements of a fete—food, drinks, decor—can be planned around the reigning spirit. Just come up with a few variations on the most obvious motifs and you're guaranteed a one-of-a-kind bash. In the following chapters, you'll meet hosts and hostesses who managed to deck their place in red, white, and blue for the Fourth without flying a single flag (see page 104) and to celebrate Thanksgiving with a spread so scrumptious, so stress-free that no one missed the turkey (see page 158).

The Bar

Let's face it: Getting your drink on is still party pastime number one. A full bar, however, isn't always the answer. If you decide to serve the hard stuff, there are

Paper products have a place in your bar setup, as long as they're as charming as this cherry cocktail napkin. But please, leave the Bounty where it belongs: under the kitchen sink.

Even the biggest boozer doesn't need a built-in bar to get by. A small cart—such as this sleek chrome Salvation Army find—will get the good times rolling.

Investing in a handsome decanter, like this bourbon pump, lets you get away with serving half-priced hooch. Over a lifetime of tippling, you'll save a ton—and guests won't know the difference.

The Cocktail Party Cheat Sheet

Alas, most guests' memories tend to be fickle. They may or may not recall your rapier wit and precious party favors, but they'll never forget—or forgive—if the drink well runs dry. While it's easy to compute the necessary number of bottles if you're serving only beer or wine, getting the ratio right on a full bar can be a real brainteaser. Hence the chart below, which estimates how much booze is required for big bashes. Of course, you may want to adjust these guidelines based on your crowd's tastes.

	NUMBER OF GUESTS			
	20–30	30–40	40–60	60–80
BEER (12-oz. bottles)	48	72	84	96
CHAMPAGNE (750-ml bottles)	4	5	6	7
DRY VERMOUTH (750-ml bottles)	1	1	2	2
RED WINE (750-ml bottles)	3	5	7	9
WHITE WINE (750-ml bottles)	6	7	8	11
BOURBON (750-ml bottles)	1	1	1	1
GIN (750-ml bottles)	1	2	2	3
RUM (750-ml bottles)	1	2	2	2
SCOTCH (750-ml bottles)	1	2	2	3
TEQUILA (750-ml bottles)	2	2	2	3
WHISKEY (750-ml bottles)	2	2	3	4
VODKA (750-ml bottles)	2	3	3	4
CLUB SODA/SELTZER (2-liter bottles)	3	3	4	5
COLA/DIET COLA (2-liter bottles)	6	7	8	9
TONIC WATER (2-liter bottles)	2	2	3	3
CRANBERRY JUICE (quarts)	2	2	6	6
GRAPEFRUIT JUICE (quarts)	2	2	3	3
ORANGE JUICE (quarts)	2	2	3	3
TOMATO JUICE (quarts)	2	2	3	3

Raising Your Basic Home Bar

Hospitality and hooch often go hand in hand, so it's a good idea to keep a few bottles around for thirsty friends who like to pop in. Of course, you don't have to shell out for Chambord or sherry (unless they're your personal faves) to stock a decent home bar. Just bag the following basics and you'll be good to flow.

SPIRITS
750 ml bourbon
750 ml gin
750 ml rum
750 ml scotch
750 ml tequila
1 liter triple sec
750 ml vodka

BEER AND WINE
2 six-packs beer
1 bottle dry vermouth
1 bottle red wine
1 bottle white wine

MIXERS
Club soda
Cola/diet cola
Ginger ale
Tonic water
Cranberry juice
Grapefruit juice
Orange juice
Tomato juice
Angostura bitters
Grenadine

GARNISHES
Celery stalks
Cocktail onions
Lemons
Limes
Olives
Salt
Sugar
Tabasco sauce
Worcestershire sauce

Source: Adapted from Bartending for Dummies, 2nd Edition (Wiley).

Elegant food can be comforting—to you and your wallet. This refined take on your mother's green bean casserole is simple to make: Toss green beans with crisped shallots and roasted shiitakes, then dress it in a mix of mustard and red wine vinegar.

a few secrets to loosening up your guests without losing your shirt at the liquor store. One holiday hostess concocted several tasty cocktails using only a single bargain bourbon (see page 174), while a different pair of party throwers offered just one specialty drink at their shindig (see page 104). Another sly—and chic—way to dress up down-market hard liquor is to decant it. Splurge on a handsome glass bottle once and you can fill it again and again with the cheap stuff.

On the other hand, if you think a Gibson's just a guitar and that Rob Roy is some movie you never saw, better stick with beer and wine. There's nothing wrong with stocking up on bottled Budweiser or even canned Hamm's, depending on the setting and the occasion. But whatever booze you choose, be sure to pick up a selection of seltzer and soft drinks for the teetotalers (or designated drivers) in the mix.

To keep the drinks flowing and the atmosphere lively, designate a bar area. You'll save yourself time and trouble by letting guests belly up and pour themselves the next round. A small steel cart, side table, butcher block, large rimmed tray—really, any sturdy surface—can be called into action. And if you're serving soft liquor only, forgo the conventional setup (and subsequent trips to the fridge) by tucking bottles into an easy-access bucket, a tub, or even an old birdbath (see page 114). Turns out, a successful bar has less to do with fancy zinc finishes and more to do with meeting supply and demand. As long as you've got enough to drink, no one will notice whether it's presented on a polished mahogany built-in or a piece of plywood atop two sawhorses.

The Food

There's no need to dial up the caterer in desperation just because you've never cracked open Julia Child's *Mastering the Art of French Cooking*. Take a look at the traditional Southern soiree on page 174 if you need convincing. How hard can it be to pour Pickapeppa sauce over a block of cream cheese? Not very. Summon your inner chef by sticking with tried-and-true recipes—a dinner party for 12 is not the time to try

💡 Taking Stock

Getting your kitchen in gear doesn't have to mean emptying your pocketbook or overcrowding your cabinets. Unless you count crème brûlée as a major food group, that $40 butane culinary torch is probably not essential. And though owning a wok, a mandoline, and a Dutch oven will make the recipes in this book easier to complete, you can always get by using a skillet, a chef's knife, and a stockpot, instead. So leave the pricey specialty items to the *Le Cordon Bleu* grads and spend your dough on the following indispensable tools of the trade.

Food Prep

BLENDER

CAN OPENER

CHEF'S KNIFE

COLANDER

GRATER

HANDHELD ELECTRIC MIXER

INSTANT-READ MEAT THER-MOMETER

LARGE METAL SPOON

MEASURING CUPS FOR DRY AND WET INGREDIENTS

MEASURING SPOONS

METAL AND RUBBER SPATULAS

NESTED MIXING BOWLS

PARING KNIFE

PEELER

PLASTIC CUTTING BOARDS (ONE EACH FOR MEAT, FISH, POULTRY, AND VEGETABLES)

ROLLING PIN

SERRATED KNIFE

WIRE WHISK

WOODEN SPOONS

Bakeware

BROWNIE PAN (9 BY 9 BY 2 INCHES)

GLASS BAKING DISH (13 BY 9 BY 2 INCHES)

LOAF PAN

METAL COOKIE SHEET

MUFFIN TIN

WIRE COOLING RACK

Stovetop

12-INCH SKILLET

2-QUART SAUCEPAN

4-QUART SAUCEPAN

8-QUART STOCKPOT

Who you callin' a couch potato? All dressed up and danced out—but not stressed out—these hosts with the most take a moment to refuel.

Channel Your Inner Cheapskate

Dream up the right theme and lowly eats can become altogether apropos. If the *Sopranos* finale is your soiree's main event, Swanson is okay, especially when served on a sectional plate atop a classic TV tray table nabbed on eBay.

out a triple reduction. Better yet, pick dishes that require more stylish assembly than actual culinary skill. You'll find that frozen pizza cut into bite-size wedges, pigs in blankets made from store-bought pastry and packaged miniwieners, and mixed salad greens from a bag are all part of the *Budget Living*–endorsed repertoire. (So, too, is fast-food take-out, especially when it's Popeyes fried chicken and biscuits or White Castle hamburgers.) Consider yourself queen of the kitchen? Well, you're still probably not rich (or foolish) enough to make filet mignon for 50. Besides, there's no shame in serving up tacos with all the fixings (see page 62). Or in taking a cue from a transplanted Kentucky boy (see page 76), who can't let Derby Day pass without putting on a raucous bash. To feed a crowd that swells with each successive year, he cooks a country ham. The cost? Just 30 bucks for a main dish that never fails to sate an army of hungry race-for-the-roses revelers.

In the end, a good party should leave you filled with food, drink, and the sort of saucy stories that'll embarrass your friends for years to come. And, heaven knows, that doesn't require a $200-an-hour event coordinator. Instead, pore over the idea-packed pages that follow. We've tapped chefs, party pros, and designers of every stripe to share their memorable menus (that don't cost much moola), their dime-store decorations (to set the mood), and their delicious drinks (to get everyone mixing). From inventive invitations to fabulously frugal favors, you'll be able to get your party started and finish it off right, having a ball all the while. Just don't worry about re-creating each of these fetes to the letter or throwing a bash every single month of the year. After all, the whole point of *Party Central* is to provide you with inspiration and information—not some intimidating agenda. Because remember: When it comes to planning, easy does it. Save the headaches for the morning after.

Swanky cocktails and sumptuous food make for a highball New Year's at a lowball price.

Adam and Sue Keller, below, raised the bar with affordable Svedka vodka and Gordon's gin. "In a mixed drink," Sue says, "I defy anyone to tell the difference from more expensive brands." Opposite: A cool gimlet was on hand to quench any thirst emergencies.

'Round Midnight

If your guests have to travel an hour to get to your house, you'd better make it worth their while. So say Sue and Adam Keller, who frequently lure New York City friends out to their Jersey City pad for soirees of such renown that when 30 people are invited, 50 show up. For this bargain New Year's blowout—think satisfying food and serious drinks for 20 or more at less than $10 a head—the Kellers originally planned to stage a 1950s shindig, replete with lounge lizard cocktails, *Father Knows Best*–style finger food, and swinging I LIKE IKE–era outfits. But the couple soon realized they were cramping their style by taking on just one decade, so they decided to mix up, quite literally, a bash for the ages.

Sue sought culinary inspiration from vintage tomes: *Betty Crocker's New Picture Cookbook* (published in 1961) and *The New Joys of Jell-O,* a '73 family heirloom. Although true gourmands might turn up their noses at her selections—cheese logs, Chex mix, Swedish meatballs, and the like—the stick-to-your-ribs spread is easy to prepare using affordable grocery-store ingredients. Plus, such hearty fare suits a night of toasting and tippling. "Those modern bits of salmon are never filling enough," Sue explains, "and people are embarrassed to eat more than one."

If the comfort food wasn't enough to put folks at ease, Sue's invitation to pose for a Polaroid was. Though she was in charge of taking each snapshot—and adding it to the ever-growing gallery of party pics that adorns one living room wall—her subjects were encouraged to "art direct" their own portraits. And by the time the film developed, most guests already had a drink in hand. To keep the tab low, Sue and Adam forwent a full bar in favor of a few special cocktails made with cost-effective Svedka vodka and Gordon's gin. As for their beer-loving friends, the Kellers asked them to bring their own. And once the swigging started, the swinging wasn't far behind.

While a "Rock Around the Clock" vibe pervaded, thanks to the full-skirted frocks worn by Sue's girlfriends, the music meandered from era to era and genre to genre. Sue's dad hit the 1880s birdcage piano with a rollicking rendition of "New York, New York." Then Adam took over at the turntable, flipping through stacks of vinyl for tunes that kept the place hopping.

As the clock neared midnight, guests took a whack at piñatas hung from the ceiling. When the goodies fell, some guests got down so intensely it was unclear when they'd actually get up. But Sue and Adam didn't mind if the celebration turned into a slumber party. After all, tomorrow would be a whole new year.

Turning the Tables

For this rockin' New Year's Eve, Adam created a musical cocktail of little-known soul songs from the '60s and '70s. The tunes have "a real funk vibe," he says, "that you can jam to even if you've never heard them before."

Cincinnati Growl ROY AYERS	**Sand Step** THE NILSMEN	**Fatback** MONGO SANTAMARIA
Tasty Cakes IDRIS MUHAMMAD	**Hung Up** SALT	**Candido's Funk** CANDIDO
Scorpio DENNIS COFFEY	**Truck Full of Soul** CARLOS MALCOLM	**Too Late** BLACK SUGAR
The Dump SOUL VIBRATIONS	**Camel Walk** THE LATINAIRES	**The Mexican Cactus** JEAN JACQUES PERREY
I Believe in Miracles THE JACKSON SISTERS	**Mercy Mercy Baby** RAY BARRETTO	**Peepin' n Hidin'** THE CORONADOS
Tick Tock Baby THE QUICKEST WAY OUT	**Subway Joe** JOE BATAAN	**Cinnamon Flower** DOM UN ROMAO
	Bang Bang CAL TJADER	

Guests partied like it was 1959 at the Kellers' Jersey City home, opposite. Above right: Adam Keller, left, and pal Rich Sanbomeno spun the night away in a booth Adam built from his dad's old engineer's desk, turntables (a wedding gift from Sue), and a collection of almost 1,000 albums.

Go that extra celebratory mile—without going broke—by handing out old-school party favors. They're still sold at throwback prices on Oriental Trading .com, where the Kellers nabbed these glow-in-the-dark glasses (12 for $4) and fringed HAPPY NEW YEAR tiaras (50 for $15), above. Opposite: A couple of foxes trotted over footprints photocopied from an old Arthur Murray dance book.

Tiny Bubbles

Instead of champagne, the Kellers prefer equally delicious but less expensive European Proseccos and Cavas. Sparkling wines by Mionetto ($15), Marqués de Gelida ($9), Bosca ($7), and Fontanafredda ($11) are great choices. (Feel like spending a little more? See page 33 for bigger-ticket bubbly.)

Develop a New Tradition—Instantly!

It's hip to be square on the Kellers' Polaroid wall of guests, which grows with each bash they throw. A cheap alternative to "real" art and a foolproof conversation starter, the collection of candids ensures that every visitor leaves a lasting impression. To start your own gallery, snap Polaroids of guests as they arrive. When it comes time to hang the portraits, Sue warns against relying on masking tape. "It only lasts about six months," she sighs. "I'm dreaming of the day I can pin each picture to the wall with tiny thumbtacks." And since there's also no use pretending Polaroid film comes cheap, stock up by the case at eCameraFilms.com, which sells bulk film at a discount.

How do you feed a crowd of
raucous revelers cheaply?
Just like June Cleaver did—by
cooking up simple yet
satisfying suburban favorites.

Betty Crocker–inspired meatballs, below, rounded out the menu. Bottom: Sue's parents, Margaret and Mike Kurta, canoodled their way into the New Year. Opposite, top: Come midnight, *girls* made passes at girls who wore glasses. Opposite, bottom: The Kellers used their stickered microwave to warm the artichoke dip.

THE RECIPES

herb cheese log
(serves 10)

- 2 8-oz. packages cream cheese
- 1 tbsp. lemon juice
- 1 clove garlic, minced
- 1 tbsp. each minced fresh thyme, oregano, and parsley
- 1 cup chopped fresh chives

Blend cream cheese, lemon juice, and garlic in a food processor or a large bowl. Mix fresh herbs on a plate or a cookie sheet. Form cream cheese mixture into a log and roll in herbs until coated. Cover with plastic wrap and chill until ready to serve with crackers and baguette slices.

nippy cheese log
(serves 10)

- 1 lb. Colby cheese, grated
- 3 oz. cream cheese
- 1 clove garlic, minced
- 1 tsp. Worcestershire sauce
- 1½ tbsp. cayenne pepper
- 1 tsp. paprika
- 1 tsp. black pepper

Blend cheeses, garlic, and Worcestershire in a food processor or a large bowl. Mix spices and spread onto a plate or a cookie sheet. Shape cheese mixture into a log and coat in spice mixture. Cover with plastic wrap and chill until ready to serve with crackers and baguette slices.

pecan cheese ball
(serves 10)

- 1 lb. cheddar cheese, grated
- 1 8-oz. package cream cheese
- 1 clove garlic, minced
- 1 tsp. chili powder
  Dash Tabasco sauce
- 2 cups chopped pecans, lightly toasted

Blend cheeses, garlic, chili powder, and Tabasco in a food processor or a large bowl. Shape mixture into a ball and coat with pecans, pressing them in gently with your hands. Cover with plastic wrap and chill until ready to serve with crackers and baguette slices.

bumps on a log
(serves 20)

- 2 large bunches celery, leaves left on
  Peanut butter (creamy/crunchy), as needed
  Raisins and/or currants, as needed

Cut base from each celery bunch and cut each stalk into thirds, leaving the leaves on the top sections. Spread peanut butter on stalks. Press raisins and/or currants into peanut butter. Arrange on a platter.

sue's tricked-out party mix
(serves 20 to 25)

- 2 sticks (16 tbsp.) unsalted butter
- 4 tbsp. Worcestershire sauce
- 2 tbsp. cayenne pepper
- 3 tsp. seasoned salt
- 1 tsp. garlic powder
- 1 tsp. onion powder
- 6 cups corn squares cereal
- 6 cups rice squares cereal
- 6 cups wheat squares cereal
- 2 cups mixed nuts
- 2 cups mini pretzels

Preheat oven to 250°F. Melt butter in a saucepan with Worcestershire. Mix spices in a bowl. Put dry ingredients (cereal, nuts, pretzels; you can also add Triscuits, Wheat Thins, Goldfish crackers, Cheese Nips, Cheerios, Melba toast rounds, etc.) into a brown paper bag. Pour a little

Worcestershire butter and spice mix in the bag and shake until evenly coated. Continue to pour small amounts of butter and spice mix into the bag, and shake until all ingredients are in the bag. Remove mixture from bag and bake for 1 hour, stirring every 15 minutes.

hot artichoke dip
(serves 20)

2 14-oz. cans artichoke hearts, drained
1 4½-oz. can chopped green chiles
1 cup mayonnaise
1 cup grated Parmesan cheese
3 cloves garlic

Pulse ingredients in a food processor—do not overmix. Place in a microwave-proof baking dish and microwave for 2 minutes, until bubbly and hot throughout, then broil for 5 minutes to brown top. Or bake at 375°F for 25 minutes. Serve with crackers and baguette slices.

swedish meatballs
(serves 20 to 25)

Meatballs*
3 lb. ground beef
1 lb. ground pork
2 tbsp. chopped onion
Vegetable oil, for browning
1 cup beef broth
2 large eggs
1 cup bread crumbs
1 tsp. pepper
2 tbsp. salt

Sauce
1 tbsp. unsalted butter
⅓ cup flour
1 tsp. paprika
1 tsp. white pepper
1 tsp. salt
1 cup beef broth
1 cup sour cream

Combine beef and pork in a bowl with a wooden spoon. Brown onion in oil and add to meat mixture along with broth, eggs, bread crumbs, pepper, and salt. With your hands, mix thoroughly until smooth. Shape into 1-inch balls. Coat a saucepan with oil and heat to medium. Brown meatballs in batches; place each batch in a large bowl when done. Leave drippings and oil in pan.

Add butter to meatball drippings and oil; over medium heat, whisk until melted. Stir in flour and seasonings until thoroughly combined. Add broth and continue whisking until gravy begins to thicken, then add sour cream. Return meatballs to the pan and stir to coat.

*For vegetarian guests, prepare store-bought meat-free balls according to package directions and substitute vegetable broth for beef broth in sauce.

chocolate fondue
(serves 20 to 25)

12 oz. unsweetened baking chocolate
3 cups sugar
2 cups heavy cream
2 sticks (16 tbsp.) unsalted butter
Pinch salt
4 tbsp. Grand Marnier (optional)

In a saucepan, melt choco-late over low heat. Add sugar, cream, butter, and salt, and stir until blended. Add Grand Marnier, if using. Transfer to a fondue pot over low heat. Serve with squares of pound cake, macaroons, pretzel rods, bananas, and straw-berries. Note: Fondue pot should be three-quarters full. Additional fondue can be covered, kept at room

Want to break the mold? Jell-O takes the cake.

THE RECEIPT

4	8-oz. packages cream cheese	$3.96
1	bunch thyme	$1.24
1	bunch oregano	$1.24
1	bunch parsley	$0.69
2	bunches chives	$3.00
2	16-oz. boxes butter crackers	$3.38
3	loaves baguette bread	$4.67
1	lb. Colby cheese	$4.23
1	lb. cheddar cheese	$2.50
1	8-oz. bag chopped pecans	$3.49
2	bunches whole celery	$2.58
1	18-oz. jar peanut butter	$1.89
1	15-oz. box raisins	$2.79
3	1/2-lb. boxes unsalted butter	$3.27
1	16-oz. box corn squares cereal	$2.49
1	15.6-oz. box rice squares cereal	$2.49
1	16-oz. box wheat squares cereal	$3.99
1	11.5-oz. can mixed nuts	$2.99
1	12-oz. bag mini pretzels	$0.50
2	14-oz. cans artichoke hearts	$3.58
1	4.5-oz. can green chiles	$1.49
1	8-oz. can grated Parmesan cheese	$2.79
3	lb. ground beef	$7.47
1	lb. ground pork	$1.39
1	small onion	$0.14
1	10.5-oz. can beef broth	$1.19
1	8-oz. can bread crumbs	$1.39
1	8-oz. carton sour cream	$0.89
2	8-oz. bars unsweetened chocolate	$5.58
1	qt. heavy cream	$2.99
1	12-oz. pound cake	$3.49
1	13-oz. box macaroons	$2.79
1	10-oz. bag pretzel rods	$1.79
1	bunch bananas	$1.29
1	pt. strawberries	$1.67
4	3-oz. boxes Jell-O	$3.00
1	8-oz. can pineapple chunks (for juice)	$1.09
1	2.6-oz. box Dream Whip dry whipped topping	$2.19
1	750-ml bottle dry vermouth	$7.99
1	1.75-l bottle gin	$18.49
1	7-oz. bottle green olives	$1.39
1	1.75-l bottle vodka	$24.99
1	1-l bottle lime juice	$5.99
2	1-l bottles ginger ale	$2.58
12	limes	$3.00

TOTAL	$162.03
(tax not included)	

ALREADY IN YOUR PANTRY: lemon juice, garlic, Worcestershire, cayenne, paprika, black pepper, chili powder, Tabasco, seasoned salt, garlic powder, onion powder, Triscuits, Wheat Thins, Goldfish crackers, Cheese Nips, Cheerios, Melba toast, mayonnaise, vegetable oil, eggs, salt, flour, white pepper, sugar, Grand Marnier
GUESTS BRING: beer

temperature, and used to replenish the pot.

crown jewel cake
(serves 20 to 25)

    1 package (3 oz.) orange Jell-O
    1 package (3 oz.) cherry Jell-O
    1 package (3 oz.) lime Jell-O
    4 cups boiling water
    1½ cups cold water
    1 package (3 oz.) lemon Jell-O
    ¼ cup sugar
    ½ cup pineapple juice
    2 envelopes Dream Whip whipped topping mix

Prepare orange, cherry, and lime Jell-O separately, using 1 cup boiling water and ½ cup cold water for each. Pour each mixture into a separate loaf pan and chill overnight. Cut into ½-inch cubes. Set aside a few cubes of each flavor for garnish.

Dissolve lemon Jell-O and sugar in 1 cup boiling water; stir in pineapple juice. Chill until slightly thickened.

Prepare whipped topping as directed on package. Blend into the thickened lemon Jell-O. Gently fold in Jell-O cubes. Spoon into a 9-inch springform pan. Chill overnight. Just before serving, run a knife around the sides of the pan to loosen the cake from the tin. Remove the springform pan. Garnish with reserved Jell-O cubes.

buckeye martini
(serves 1)

    ½ oz. dry vermouth
    3 oz. gin
    Green olive

In a cocktail shaker filled with ice, combine vermouth and gin. Shake well and strain into a martini glass. Garnish with a green olive.

groovy gimlet
(serves 1)

    Sugar
    2¼ oz. gin or vodka
    ¾ oz. Rose's lime juice

Dip the moistened rim of a glass into sugar. In a cocktail shaker filled with ice, combine gin or vodka with lime juice. Shake and strain into the glass.

mod mule
(serves 1)

    1½ oz. vodka
    Ginger ale
    Lime wedge

Fill a highball glass with crushed ice. Add vodka, then ginger ale. Garnish with a lime wedge.

Midnight Specials: Seven Smart Buys and a Splurge

If you're hosting more than 20 guests, you'll probably want to stick with the Kellers' $15-and-under sparkling wine suggestions (page 26). But for more intimate gatherings, you can up the ante without overspending. According to Eric Macaire, co-owner of two champagne bars—the Bubble lounges in New York and San Francisco—there's some middle ground between André and Cristal. The proof: his seven priced-right picks (plus one worthy splurge), below.

1. CHAMPAGNE NICOLAS FEUILLATTE BRUT ($21): Deliciously floral, light-bodied, and wonderfully subtle yet effervescent—a genuine French champagne for less than $25!

2. ROEDERER ESTATE ROSÉ BRUT ($20): The folks who charge $300 for Cristal Rosé champagne also make this dry, plummy sparkling wine at their second vineyard in California.

3. BOLLINGER SPECIAL CUVÉE BRUT ($32): Bond drank it in *Goldeneye* and *Tomorrow Never Dies,* and after a few sips of this pinot noir–style champagne, you'll hope tomorrow never comes.

4. IRON HORSE CLASSIC VINTAGE BRUT ($28): This creamy California sparkler has been uncorked at White House state dinners since 1985, giving rise to especially spirited political debates.

5. POL ROGER BRUT ($24): "In defeat I need it; in victory I deserve it," Winston Churchill said of this robust champagne. He carried it into war zones, but luckily you don't have to risk your life to sip it.

6. LAURENT-PERRIER CUVÉE ROSÉ BRUT ($43): A favorite of Prince Charles, this renowned rosé champagne is brisk and complex, rich with notes of berries and honeysuckle.

7. TAITTINGER LA FRANÇAISE BRUT ($28): An ethereally airy champagne made with a high percentage of delicate chardonnay.

8. PERRIER JOUËT FLEUR DE CHAMPAGNE ($86): Okay, you could get a few of the others for the price of this French classic, but the divine 1995 vintage is worth the indulgence for a special occasion.

1.

2.

3.

4.

5.

6.

7.

8.

Stick It to Tradition

Think piñata bashing is child's play? The Kellers' adult guests, above, enjoyed taking a swing at four big numbers (one 2, two 0s, you get the idea…), which cost around $15 each at ThePinataStore .com. Opposite: Inside each piñata was a mix of kiddie treats and grown-up goodies. The mini booze bottles (made of plastic) are available at most liquor stores; both OrientalTrading.com and USToy.com sell cheap trinkets and candy in bulk.

Hangover Helpers

If ringing in the New Year has left you with a little ringing in the head, try one of these methods for muting the bells:

1. WICKED LITTLE PILL Hollywood's cocktail cure of choice, RU-21 (ingredients include vitamins and natural compounds), is said to preclude post-partying pain. (www.clubru21.com)

2. WATER, WATER EVERYWHERE Sue Keller swears by six ounces of prevention (water) for every six-ounce drink. Adam simply avoids sugary cocktails altogether.

3. GREASE IS THE WORD Head straight to McDonald's. Order the Egg McMuffin Extra Value Meal. And supersize it.

4. HAIR OF THE DOG Start with a vitamin-rich glass of tomato juice. Blend in Tabasco, Worcestershire, and horseradish to taste. Add a shot of vodka.

Febr

uary

Single on Valentine's Day?
Throw our budget bash for the
unattached and you'll get by—
with a little help from your friends.

The Lonely Hearts Club Brunch

THE MENU
cheese straws
ruby red fruit salad
wasabi bacon
cornmeal waffles
home-cured gravlax
bagels and herb cream cheese
potato-zucchini pancakes
chocolate-dipped strawberries
strawberry sparklers
blood orange mimosas
bloody marvelous bloody marys

Normally, Valentine's Day is marked by either doily-draped, couples-only snuggle-fests or sad-sack single-tons gathering over stiff martinis. But New Yorker Demi Adeniran found a very happy medium. Having grown weary of hearing single girlfriends complain about the dearth of dateable men, she decided that "it was time to get proactive and quit whining." Her solution? Invite eight unattached gals over for a brunch mixer with a clever twist: Each guest was required to bring along a single, straight man—someone she adores "in a strictly nonromantic way." The thinking being that even if your guy friend wasn't *your* soul mate, perhaps sparks would fly between him and another one of the ladies.

The bubbly hostess, below, saved money by subbing sparkling wine for champagne. Opposite: Heart-shaped boxes filled with wry BitterSweets ($16 for two boxes; www.despair.com) give the holiday a hearty wink.

💡 Prelude to a Kiss

Having trouble coaxing those shy singles to mingle? Follow Adeniran's lead and resurrect some junior high party stunts for all their touchy-feely potential. Pass the Orange, above, practically redefines necking, as a citrus is transferred from chin to chin. Opposite: After that coy warm-up, it's a short jump to the kissy coed coupler, Spin the Bottle.

An interior designer by trade, Adeniran is used to paying attention to detail—with the emphasis on *paying*. But for this party, less was definitely more. "Limiting your budget forces you to get creative," she says. By using her own mismatched china and fashioning napkins from fabric scraps, she saved enough to splurge on a few great accents—including classic candy favors and two dozen roses (purchased as buds a week in advance to avoid the holiday's inevitable price hike).

If the flowers and delicate dishes served as a nod to tradition, Adeniran's menu added sufficient spice to the sweet scene. Humdrum breakfast staples got a new spin from fresh flavors, like cornmeal-spiked waffles and bacon glazed in wasabi paste. A pal even offered his gravlax recipe, so instead of blowing $16 a pound for a store-bought version of the Scandinavian treat, she cured her own, less expensive fresh fillets at home. As for stocking the bar, Adeniran scrimped on no-name vodka for the Bloody Marys and swapped sparkling wine for chichi champagne as a mixer for the lighter, fruitier cocktails.

The hostess waited until everyone was happily sated before she broke the ice with a round of speed dating and some risqué party games, such as Spin the Bottle. As the afternoon wound down, each guest dropped Adeniran a note detailing his or her incipient crushes— Cupid's work is never done—and she promised to facilitate the rendezvous. (As a result, at least one couple is happily brunching à deux these days.)

In the end, Adeniran's smart soiree proved that while anyone carrying a bouquet and a box of Godiva can offer a Valentine's Day with heart, it takes a little more to have one with a pulse. A few smooches, some tasty nibbles, and a bit of faux bubbly sweetened the afternoon for these singles—no soaring violins necessary.

The invitations, left, let guests know that "just friends" was just the ticket. All it took to create the heart-to-heart effect was some construction paper, a silver paint pen, and a few idle hours. What's not to love?

Take Me—I'm Yours!

Instead of throwaway decorations, Adeniran used tchotchkes that did double duty: During the party, red foil bags filled with kitschy tokens—including vintage love guides by Accoutrements ($2 each at ZooMagoo.com) and Grow a Girlfriend (or Boy-friend) dolls ($3.50 each; www.seefred.com)—added a dash of color to the mantel; afterward Adeniran's guests took the items home as favors.

Love on the Run

To ensure that guests put their best faces forward at the party, Adeniran arranged a round of speed dating. Each lonely heart gave a brief bio before the entire group—I'm a Scorpio, I like piña coladas and getting caught in the rain—then the gang paired off for one-on-one conversations, switching partners every two minutes until everyone had a chance to flirt with everyone else.

Strawberry garnish, bloody marys, and mimosas gave the bash a rosy glow.

Pucker up! A tangy mix of blood oranges and blackberries provided a perfect pregame prep.

THE RECIPES

cheese straws
(makes about 20 straws)

- 1 16- to 18-oz. package frozen puff pastry, thawed (2 sheets)
- 1 slightly beaten egg white
- 1 tsp. freshly ground black pepper
- 1½ cups sharp white cheddar, shredded

Preheat oven to 375°F. Line a baking sheet with parchment paper and set aside. Unfold puff pastry onto a lightly floured surface; brush it with a layer of beaten egg white. Sprinkle half of the pepper and half of the cheese over pastry. Top with second sheet of puff pastry. Brush with another layer of egg white and sprinkle with remaining pepper and cheese. With a rolling pin, roll out pastry so that the two sheets stick together. Now, cut rolled pastry into ½-inch strips. Gently twist each strip several times, lay each one on the baking sheet, and press the ends down to secure the twists. Bake for 18 minutes, or until golden brown. Transfer straws to a wire rack to cool.

ruby red fruit salad
(serves 16)

- 2 cups halved and hulled strawberries
- 2 cups peeled and sectioned blood orange
- 2 cups blackberries
- 2 cups peeled and diced cantaloupe
- 1 tbsp. confectioners' sugar

Combine fruits in a large bowl and toss with confectioners' sugar. Cover and chill until ready to serve, up to 6 hours.

wasabi bacon
(serves about 20)

- 2 1-lb. packages bacon
- 1 1½-oz. tube prepared wasabi paste

Cook bacon in a large heavy skillet over medium heat, turning occasionally, until crisp. Transfer bacon to a paper-towel-lined plate to drain. Dot each strip lightly with wasabi paste, and spread it along each strip with a butter knife if desired.

cornmeal waffles
(makes 18)

- 1 cup vegetable oil
- 1 cup Jiffy corn muffin mix
- 5 cups Aunt Jemima Pancake & Waffle Mix
- 3 eggs
- 4½ cups milk

Grease waffle iron with 1 tbsp. vegetable oil. (Adeniran used a heart-shaped version, available at Cooking .com for around $40.) In a large bowl, combine corn muffin mix and pancake mix. Whisk eggs and remaining oil together in a separate bowl. Stir eggs and oil into corn muffin–pancake mixture; then add milk and continue to stir until lumps disappear. Let sit 5 minutes. Spoon batter into hot waffle iron and cook until golden brown. Keep waffles warm on a baking sheet in a 200°F oven until they're ready to serve.

Home-cured gravlax and cream cheese spiked with herbs put a fresh spin on the typical brunch menu.

Store-bought chocolate can be impersonal—and pricey. Opt for a D.I.Y. dessert.

THE RECEIPT

1	16-oz. package frozen puff pastry	$3.49
1	dozen jumbo eggs	$1.69
8	oz. sharp white cheddar	$2.50
3	16-oz. boxes strawberries	$8.97
17	blood oranges	$9.35
4	1/2-pt. blackberries	$10.00
1	cantaloupe	$2.49
2	1-lb. packages bacon	$7.98
1	1.5-oz. tube prepared wasabi paste	$2.59
1	8.5-oz. box Jiffy corn muffin mix	$0.59
1	32-oz. box Aunt Jemima Pancake & Waffle Mix	$2.29
1/2	gal. whole milk	$2.49
2	bunches dill	$2.98
2.5	lb. salmon fillets	$15.45
1	small white onion	$0.75
1	bunch fresh chives	$1.99
2	lemons	$0.78
2	8-oz. bricks cream cheese	$4.18
18	assorted bagels	$5.85
1	lb. Yukon gold potatoes	$0.99
1	lb. zucchini	$1.49
1	11-oz. can corn	$0.89
1	12-oz. bag semisweet chocolate chips	$2.69
6	oz. white chocolate	$2.50
1	10-oz. package frozen strawberries	$2.29
3	750-ml bottle sparkling white wine	$14.97
2	1-l bottle Bloody Mary mix	$7.98
8	limes	$2.00
1	1.75-l bottle vodka	$24.99
1	bunch celery	$1.29

TOTAL   **$148.49**
(tax not included)

ALREADY IN YOUR PANTRY: pepper, confectioners' sugar, vegetable oil, kosher salt, brown sugar, peppercorns, salt, flour, horse-radish, Worcestershire, Tabasco

home-cured gravlax
(serves 20)

- ⅓ cup kosher salt
- ⅓ cup brown sugar
- 2 tbsp. black peppercorns
- 1 bunch dill
- 2½ lb. salmon (2 fillets of roughly the same size)

Mix together kosher salt and brown sugar, and set aside. Use a mortar and pestle to coarsely grind peppercorns. Rinse, dry, and coarsely chop dill, discarding any stems. Pat fillets dry and place them flesh side up on a sheet of plastic wrap. Cover both pieces with salt-sugar mixture and sprinkle with pepper. Cover one piece of salmon with dill and use the plastic wrap to flip the other piece on top to sandwich dill (do it quickly, so you don't lose the mixture). Wrap salmon tightly in plastic wrap, then in foil. Place in a shallow dish and put a weight (like a heavy book) on top. Refrigerate for 4 days. Unwrap and wipe off excess sugar-salt mixture, pepper, and dill. For best texture, air-dry fish in refrigerator on a wire rack (though a regular plate works, too) for another day. When ready to serve, use a sharp knife to slice gravlax on an angle (slices should be paper-thin).

bagels and herb cream cheese
(serves 16)

- 1 tbsp. minced fresh dill
- 1 small white onion, finely chopped
- 1 tbsp. fresh chives, finely chopped, plus ½ tsp. for garnish
- 2 lemons, zested
- 2 8-oz. packages cream cheese, softened
  Salt and pepper, to taste
- 18 assorted bagels

Fold dill, onion, chives, and lemon zest into softened cream cheese, season with salt and pepper, and stir until well blended. Chill 1 hour to let flavors develop, or overnight. Garnish with chopped chives. Serve with bagels and gravlax (see recipe at left).

potato-zucchini pancakes
(makes about 20)

- 1 lb. Yukon gold potatoes
- 1 lb. fresh zucchini
- ½ cup canned whole kernel corn
- 3 eggs, beaten
- ¼ tsp. salt
- ¼ cup flour
  Vegetable oil, as needed

Peel and julienne potatoes. (A mandoline is ideal for this task; Bed Bath & Beyond carries a Zyliss version for $50.) Place potatoes in a bowl, add water until just covered, and set aside. Julienne zucchini and place in a large bowl. Drain and rinse corn, and add to zucchini. Drain potatoes in a sieve, shaking out excess water, and place in the bowl with zucchini and corn. Pour eggs over vegetables and stir to coat. In a separate bowl, add salt to flour, then gradually add dry ingredients to vegetable mixture. At this point, vegetables will begin to stick together. Generously coat a large heavy-bottomed skillet with oil and place over medium heat. Once oil is hot, scoop enough mixture to form 2- to 3-inch-diameter circles into the pan. (Mixture will be loose; the heat will form it into a patty.) Fry until crisp and golden, about 2 to 3 minutes per side. Drain on a paper-towel-lined plate.

chocolate-dipped strawberries
(makes 24)

- 24 strawberries
- 1 cup semisweet chocolate chips
- 6 oz. white chocolate, chopped

Rinse and thoroughly dry strawberries. Line a baking sheet with wax or parchment paper. Place semisweet chips in the top of a double boiler; heat and stir until smooth. Remove from heat. Dip 12 strawberries halfway into melted chocolate. Gently shake off any excess and place berries on the baking sheet. Repeat these steps with white chocolate and remaining strawberries. Place baking sheet in refrigerator and let chill until chocolate is set, at least 30 minutes, or overnight.

strawberry sparklers
(serves 8)

- 1 10-oz. package frozen strawberries, thawed
- 1 750-ml bottle sparkling white wine
- 4 fresh strawberries, hulled and halved

Puree thawed strawberries and ¼ cup sparkling wine in a blender or a food processor. Pour remaining sparkling wine into eight champagne flutes, gently spoon 2 to 3 tsp. strawberry puree into each glass, and stir. Float half a strawberry in each drink for garnish.

blood orange mimosa
(serves 1)

- ¼ cup blood orange juice
- 4 oz. sparkling white wine
- 1 slice blood orange

Place ice cubes in an 8-oz. wineglass, add blood orange juice, slowly pour in sparkling wine, and stir. Garnish with a thin slice of blood orange.

bloody marvelous bloody marys
(serves 8)

- 1 1-l bottle Bloody Mary mix
- 1½ tbsp. horseradish, drained
- 1 tbsp. Worcestershire sauce
- 4 limes, juiced
- 2 cups vodka
  Salt and pepper, to taste
  Tabasco sauce, to taste
- 1 bunch celery, rinsed and cut into sticks

Combine Bloody Mary mix, horseradish, Worcestershire, lime juice, and vodka in a pitcher. Season with salt, pepper, and Tabasco. Garnish each drink with a celery stick.

Adeniran saved enough money on her party prep to splurge on a heart-shaped waffle iron.

A simple concoction of strawberry puree and sparkling wine helped guests loosen up.

Ma

rch

OSCAR NIGHT

753003

753003

Who says you can't throw a blockbuster Academy Awards bash on an indie-flick budget?

Reel 'em in with a great invitation, below. These film canister invites from PlumParty.com aren't cheap at five for $18, but they are easy: Just scrawl the party details on the film with a Sharpie and pop into a padded mailer. Opposite: A faux Marilyn Monroe and James Dean mug for the camera.

ONE STARRY NIGHT

Whoever said that sitting around watching the tube is antisocial must spend Oscar night glued to C-SPAN. The Academy Awards is the one occasion each year that elevates television to the level of a can't-miss celebration. And not just for show-biz glitterati—ever since the ceremony was first televised in 1953, we ordinary folk have been in on the fun. Our idea of the perfect Oscar party? A star-studded Hollywood story shot through the lens of cinematic camp. Witness the costume drama and movie trappings we used to transform a loft apartment into an ersatz theater. It took some effort, sure, but still left plenty of time for chatting up 10 or 15 friends, dressed as their favorite characters.

FACE TIME

How do you get Bette Davis, Warren Beatty, and Peter O'Toole, opposite, to clean up during dinner? Simply download vintage images, print them out on transfer paper (about $12 for 10 sheets at office-supply stores), and iron them on to cloth napkins (these cost less than $3 each at Bed, Bath & Beyond). The same pics can bring star power to coasters: Mount three-by-three-inch color copies onto four-inch squares of construction paper, then encase them between self-laminating sheets (also available at office-supply stores; 10 for $6).

Marilyn Monroe and James Dean arrived together, while Mahatma Gandhi put nonviolence aside to pal around with Maximus from *Gladiator*. Costumes were encouraged, though not mandatory. Same went for playing Oscar-themed games like movie-star Twister. In fact, about the only things required for this bash were keeping the costs down and the kitsch factor up. It took just a few hours of D.I.Y. decorating to create the set: Asian lanterns acted as houselights for a faux Grauman's Chinese Theatre, complete with stage curtains and a rented projector. Snapshots of movie icons, cut from picture books or bought online, played multiple parts—laminated into coasters, ironed on napkins, and taped atop the aforementioned Twister mat.

The theater motif also led to sly spins on concession-stand fare: Pigs in Blankets replaced hot dogs; cheese fondue stood in for nachos; and pretzels got a kick from not just mustard but four other sweet and savory sauces. As for drinks? Spiked slushies, water, Coke, and, in honor of Hollywood royalty, the King of Beers.

Vanity Fair's high-society fete it wasn't. Instead, this event was more akin to the inaugural Academy Awards ceremony in 1929, which was light on pomp, but not on partying—essentially, a casually debauched dinner affair among friends. Besides, haven't you always wanted to say, "Hey, Gandhi, pass me a Bud."

Do the Twist

As a movie, *Twister* sort of, um, blew, but the game is perfect for the mid-Oscar lull. Give it a cinematic spin by covering the colored circles with silver-screen icons (and writing their names on the accompanying spinner). Reduce or enlarge the portraits so that the stars' heads fill the six-inch circles. Then tape the printouts to the mat in the manner shown above. Extra points if you can say, "I've got my left foot on Daniel Day-Lewis."

Nothing says "the movies" like popcorn, especially when it's served in classic boxes straight out of an RKO. These run about $13 for 50 at HomeTheater Supplies.com, which ships gratis in the continental U.S., so you can offer free refills to any hungry *Urban Cowboy.*

THE CURTAIN CALL

A 19-inch screen may be fine for you, but your guests will have a hard enough time as it is squinting to see J. Lo's low-cut outfit. That's where the rented TV projector comes in. It's a splurge at about $100 a day (plus $35 shipping each way) from Rent Quick.com, but ask around—you might be able to borrow one from, say, a local school's AV club. Either way, it's worth the effort; most projectors plug right into your cable box or VCR, turning any blank wall into movie magic. Increase the drama by hanging red fabric on either side of the picture, and make sure there's plenty of comfortable seating—if not actual seats—by breaking out some beanbag chairs and floor cushions. Then, for a Grauman's Chinese Theatre feel, add some Asian pillowcases ($15 and up) and a few nylon hanging lanterns ($7 to $11), all available at PearlRiver.com.

LIVE

Here's looki at you Kid

Leave the gun Take the cannolis

Mary Jane

Nominated for best cocktail: This *Ice Storm*. Affordable Kool-Aid–based slushies (see page 61 for a full recipe), above, bring the taste of the multiplex's Slush Puppies to your home theater. But these flavors are rated for adults only; each drink is spiked with a shot of vodka.

The Sweets Hereafter .

Even grown-ups linger at the candy counter, so let them act like…yes, kids in a candy shop. Buy concession-stand classics such as Mary Janes, Good & Plentys, Jujyfruits, Twizzlers, and Raisinets, opposite, in bulk at Costco, Target, or at DiscountCandy.com, then set the goodies out in paint-mixing pails equipped with pet-food scoops—all unused, of course! To turn the sugary stashes into party favors, provide guests with Chinese take-out boxes (many Asian restaurants will sell them to you cheap), adorned with favorite film quotes.

There's nothing mystic about this pizza, left. Simply heat up frozen pies (see page 60 for five tasty options) and cut them into bite-size pieces. To make things even easier, avoid fridge duty by setting out beer, soda, and bottled water in galvanized tubs (these were less than $10 each at Lowe's). Opposite, left: Guests go hog wild for Pigs in Blankets. Opposite, right: There's something about Mary Poppins, who shares a joke with Forrest Gump.

THE RECIPES

caramel popcorn
(serves 6 to 8)
8–10 cups freshly popped popcorn
Cooking spray, as needed
1 cup dry-roasted unsalted peanuts
1 cup brown sugar
1 stick (8 tbsp.) unsalted butter
3 tbsp. light corn syrup
½ tsp. ground cinnamon

Remove any unpopped kernels from popcorn. Preheat oven to 325°F. Coat two 9-by-13-inch glass baking dishes with cooking spray, and divide popcorn and peanuts between them.

In a heavy saucepan over medium-low heat, combine brown sugar, butter, corn syrup, and cinnamon, and cook until butter melts. Simmer, stirring, for 3 minutes to make caramel.

Pour caramel over popcorn and peanuts. Using a spoon coated with cooking spray, stir until coated with caramel. Bake, stirring once, for 20 minutes. Meanwhile, coat several pieces of parchment paper with cooking spray.

Turn warm caramel corn out onto paper in a single layer and let cool. Popcorn will remain crisp in an airtight container for up to 5 days.

parmesan popcorn
(serves 6 to 8)
8–10 cups freshly popped popcorn
3 tbsp. unsalted butter
½ tsp. salt
½ cup Parmesan cheese, grated

Remove any unpopped kernels and place popcorn in a large bowl. Preheat oven to 350° F. Line two cookie

sheets with parchment paper.

In a small saucepan, melt butter over low heat, then whisk in salt and ¼ cup cheese. Remove from heat, pour mixture over popcorn, and stir until coated. Add remaining ¼ cup cheese and mix well. Spread popcorn onto baking sheets in a single layer and crisp in oven for 10 minutes, or until cheese is slightly golden. Popcorn will stay crisp in an airtight container for up to 2 days.

chili-lime popcorn
(serves 6 to 8)
8–10 cups freshly popped popcorn
½ tsp. salt
2 tsp. chili powder
Dash cayenne pepper
3 tbsp. unsalted butter
½ lime, juiced

Remove any unpopped

kernels and place popcorn in a large bowl. In a separate small bowl, mix together salt, chili powder, and cayenne.

In a small saucepan, melt butter over low heat. Add lime juice and allow mixture to boil, whisking, for 1 to 1½ minutes. Remove from heat and drizzle over popcorn, tossing to coat.

Sprinkle half of the spice mixture over buttered popcorn, then stir until evenly coated. Repeat with remaining spice mixture. Popcorn will stay crisp in an airtight container for up to 2 days.

mini pretzels
(makes 25 2-inch pretzels)
1 package rapid-rise yeast
2½ cups all-purpose flour, plus additional ¼ to ½ cup

1½ tsp. sugar
1 tsp. salt
½ cup whole milk
3 tsp. unsalted butter
½ cup hot water
1 egg
Cinnamon and sugar, sesame seeds, or coarse salt, for toppings

In a large mixing bowl, combine yeast, 2½ cups flour, sugar, and salt. Set aside. In a 2-cup glass measuring cup, heat milk and butter in microwave until butter melts. Add hot water, then pour liquid into dry ingredients, beating with an electric mixer until dough just comes together and is tacky.

Turn dough out onto a clean surface and gradually add ¼ to ½ cup remaining flour, kneading by hand, until dough is no longer tacky. Continue kneading for 10 minutes. Cover dough with plastic wrap and let rest in a warm place for 10 minutes to rise.

Cut the dough into 1-tbsp. portions and roll into 8-inch long strips. Curve the ends downward, then cross them as you bring them up again, pressing ends into opposite sides of the top of the pretzel (see photo on page 61). Place pretzels seam side down on a parchment-covered baking sheet. Cover with plastic wrap and allow dough to rise until doubled in size, about 25 to 30 minutes. Meanwhile, preheat oven to 350°F.

In a small bowl, beat egg lightly with 1 tbsp. water. Brush pretzels lightly with egg wash and sprinkle with desired toppings. Bake until golden, 15 to 20 minutes. Serve warm.

spicy marinara dipping sauce
(makes 2½ cups)

2 cloves garlic, minced
2 tbsp. olive oil
1 tsp. dried basil
1 tsp. crushed red pepper
1 tsp. salt
1 tsp. sugar
1 6-oz. can tomato paste
1 28-oz. can crushed tomatoes

In a small saucepan over a medium-low flame, heat garlic in olive oil until sizzling and fragrant. Add remaining ingredients and ½ cup water, and bring to a boil. Reduce heat to low and simmer, uncovered, until reduced by nearly half, about 15 minutes. Stir occasionally to prevent sauce from sticking to the pan. Allow sauce to cool, then refrigerate overnight. Reheat and serve warm.

asian dipping sauce
(makes 1 cup)

2 tbsp. finely chopped green onion
1 2-inch knob of ginger, peeled and minced
2 tbsp. sesame oil
6 tbsp. rice wine vinegar
⅔ cup Japanese soy sauce (shoyu)
¼ tsp. chili oil

Combine all ingredients in a small bowl; mix thoroughly.

mustard-onion dipping sauce
(makes 1 cup)

2 4-oz. jars Inglehoffer Stone Ground mustard
2 tsp. very finely diced sweet onion

Spoon mustard into serving dish; sprinkle onion on top.

citrus cream cheese dip (makes 1 cup)

1 cup cream cheese
2 tsp. finely grated lemon or orange zest
2 tsp. honey

AND THE OSCAR GOES TO...

Our nominees for best performance in a frozen pizza are:

1. FRESCHETTA SUPREME PIZZA ($6; 30.64 oz.) Ah, special effects. Convincing faux-fresh features and a perfectly balanced sauce make this a winner in two categories: best looking and best tasting.

2. CELESTE PIZZA FOR ONE ($2; 5.58 oz.): The sauce is the star in this satisfying solo show. But you may want to wolf down Celeste's topping—nubby pepperoni fragments—without examining them.

3. RED BARON PIZZERIA STYLE PIZZA ($6; 29.45 oz.): This ersatz ensemble of sauce, pepperoni, and dough is mighty tasty, but authentic? It's to pizzeria pizza what a Lender's is to a deli bagel.

4. TONY'S THIN CRUST PIZZA ($2.50; 14.20 oz.): Shallowness (of crust) is a plus in this surprisingly good, basic pizza pie—Tony's takes top honors in the crispy crust category.

5. TOTINO'S CRISP CRUST PARTY PIZZA (1.50; 9.8 oz.): Why'd we serve Totino's? It's dirt cheap, and with each successive beer, the flimsy crust, sugary sauce, and "mock"-zzerella get more irresistible.

1.

2.

3.

4.

5.

Guests cannot live by bread alone, so serve pretzels with a plethora of sauces.

Combine all ingredients in a bowl; mix thoroughly.

sugar and spice butter
(makes about ⅔ cup)

- 10 tbsp. unsalted butter, slightly softened
- 4 tbsp. brown sugar
- ¼ tsp. grated nutmeg
- ½ tsp. ground cloves
- 1 tsp. ground cinnamon

In a small bowl, mix together butter and sugar, beating with a spoon to combine. Stir in spices. Refrigerate until ready to serve.

pigs in blankets
(makes about 45)

- 1 8-oz. can Pillsbury Crescent Rolls
- 1 16-oz. package mini wieners

Preheat the oven to 375ºF. Cut each crescent roll triangle into five or six smaller triangles. Wrap one around each wiener, arrange on a sheet pan, and bake for about 15 minutes.

garlic cheese fondue
(serves 6 to 8)

- 1 clove garlic, peeled and split
- 1½ cups dry white wine
- ½ cup whole milk
- ¾ lb. Swiss cheese, grated
- ¼ lb. Parmesan cheese, grated
- 2 tsp. cornstarch
- 2 tbsp. water or brandy
- 2 tbsp. unsalted butter
  Salt and cayenne

- pepper, to taste
- 2 baguettes, cubed

Rub garlic inside the bottom of a medium-size earthenware pot and place over medium heat. Discard garlic.

Add wine, milk, and both cheeses, and stir until cheese melts and mixture is well combined, 5 to 7 minutes. Place cornstarch in a cup, whisk in water (or brandy), then add to cheese mixture. Simmer, stirring, until thickened, about 5 minutes. Stir in butter and season with salt and cayenne. Pour into a fondue pot or chafing dish. Serve with baguette cubes for dipping.

slushies
(makes four 8-oz. drinks)

- 4 cups ice
- ¾ cup Kool-Aid Sugar-Sweetened Drink Mix, any flavor
- ½ cup vodka (or to taste)

In a blender, combine 2 cups ice, Kool-Aid, ½ cup water, and vodka. Pulse to combine. Add remaining 2 cups ice; continue to blend until you achieve a slushlike consistency. Serve immediately. For other varieties of slushies, substitute an alternative flavor Kool-Aid mix and repeat.

THE RECEIPT

1 32-oz. package popcorn kernels	$1.59
1 16-oz. jar dry-roasted unsalted peanuts	$3.09
1 1-lb. box brown sugar	$0.89
1 1-lb. box unsalted butter	$3.89
3/4 lb. Parmesan cheese	$5.25
1 lime	$0.25
1 3-pack rapid-rise yeast	$1.89
1 1-lb. bag all-purpose flour	$1.09
1 2-oz. package sesame seeds	$3.99
1 6-oz. can tomato paste	$0.59
1 28-oz. can crushed tomatoes	$2.79
1 bunch green onion	$0.49
1/4 lb. knob ginger	$0.45
1 6-oz. bottle sesame oil	$2.19
1 20.2-oz. bottle rice wine vinegar	$1.95
1 10-oz. bottle Japanese soy sauce (shoyu)	$3.59
1 8.5-oz. bottle chili oil	$3.29
2 4-oz. jars Inglehoffer Stone Ground mustard	$3.58
1 sweet onion	$0.36
1 8-oz. block cream cheese	$1.19
2 lemons	$0.78
1 8-oz. can Pillsbury Crescent Rolls	$1.49
1 16-oz. package mini wieners	$3.49
1 750-ml bottle dry white wine	$4.99
3/4 lb. Swiss cheese	$4.49
2 baguettes	$4.38
6 10-oz. frozen pizzas	$9.00
5 bulk packages assorted candy	$51.95
3 19-oz. canisters Kool-Aid	$10.47
1 750-ml bottle vodka	$7.99
1 24-bottle case water	$5.99
2 6-packs Coke, in bottles	$9.18
2 6-packs Diet Coke, in bottles	$9.18
4 12-packs 12-oz. Budweiser longnecks	$39.96
TOTAL	**$205.74**
(tax not included)	

ALREADY IN YOUR PANTRY: cooking spray, light corn syrup, cinnamon, salt, chili powder, cayenne, sugar, milk, egg, coarse salt, garlic, olive oil, basil, crushed red pepper, honey, nutmeg, cloves, cornstarch, brandy

Ebony Snow Hurr steps to the music while her hubby, Joe Brody, keeps the conga beat.

Potluck, *Por Favor*

There's no denying that a potluck party brings a lot to the table: a smaller price tag, less time spent in the kitchen—and, quite possibly, 10 tuna casseroles. Too chancy? Chicago stationery designer Ebony Snow Hurr thought so as she and husband Joe Brody were planning their annual Adios to Winter soiree. A self-confessed control freak, Hurr sees entertaining as performance art, where every detail is important enough to be scripted. But as a consummate party girl who hosts a dozen fetes a year, she found it hard to resist the potluck's casual, communal vibe—not to mention its affordable aspects. Hurr's clever compromise: Instead of having her 12 or so friends labor to bring finished dishes, she asked them to arrive with specific dinner ingredients—all cheaper than the typical bottle of wine. While this it-takes-a-village-to-make-a-meal approach wouldn't work with, say, a menu of Stroganoff or slow-roasted rack of lamb (who wants to eat at 3 A.M.?), it's perfect for a taco bar, which requires partygoers to assemble their meals on the spot. Hurr made the minimal prep

THE MENU
roasted corn salsas
gringo guacamole
tamales
taco bar
mexican soda
and beer
lake michigan
margaritas
shaved ice

Two hands are better than one, but 12 really rock! Because Mexican dishes require lots of slicing and dicing, the hostess, above holding a pitcher, turned the task into a party icebreaker, handing out cutting boards and knives. And, of course, cocktails.

work—shredding lettuce, dicing tomatoes, grating cheese—a part of the party, with friends forming a culinary conga line that combined chatting and chopping. "Everyone ends up hanging in the kitchen as it is," she says. "So why not make it the focal point?"

Even better, the south-of-the-border smorgasbord gave Hurr a hook for the event. "All my parties have a distinct theme," the Art Institute of Chicago grad says, "something to plan around." To set the tone for this one, she put out colorful dollar-store platters and scattered vivid paper flowers everywhere, transforming her pad into a slice of Mexicali on the Midway.

Of course, once the guests arrived, the hosts didn't treat them like galley slaves. Far from it. Hurr and Brody had already roasted corn for salsa, made chicken taco filling, and set out cheap, tasty store-bought tamales. As their crew chopped, Hurr fortified them with Lake Michigan Margaritas, Mexican sodas (as cheap as Pepsis but with much more personality), and *cervezas*. And naturally, everyone ate, gorging on the fruit of their collective labor. Dessert was kept on ice— literally—in the form of shaved ice topped with grenadine or lime syrup and an optional dash of tequila.

Spurred to action by the spiked snow cones and margaritas, *los invitados* kicked up their heels on the dance floor. And when they got really silly, Hurr had them record it for posterity. Long a fan of photo booths, she set up one of her own with a digital camera, so revelers could take candid shots. By the time this party of the people started breaking up, no one had done more work than Hurr herself—but no one had danced, drank, or reveled more, either. *¡Viva la potluck!*

So Bloomin' Easy

FOR A STATIONERY DESIGNER like Hurr, making her studio into a garden of paper flowers was an essential—but not taxing—task. In fact, all you need to put your mettle into these petals is colored tissue paper (about $5 for 60 sheets at art-supply stores), the ability to use a pair of scissors, and all of about 10 minutes (see below). Then try adding simple flourishes, like painting the blossom edges with food coloring.

1. STACK six to eight sheets of tissue paper and cut into 10-by-12-inch rectangles.

2. FOLD each cut stack like an accordion and wrap a pipe cleaner around its center.

3. CUT along the edges of the stacks to create pointed or rounded petals.

4. PULL each sheet up toward the flower's center to shape the blooms.

You don't need a green thumb (or much green) to decorate with Hurr's easily crafted paper blooms.

Loco for the Lens

What do babies, puppies, and photo booths have in common? They're all capable of robbing otherwise dignified adults of their inhibitions. The photo booth seemed to fit the bill at Hurr's saucy spring celebration, inspiring folks to let their hair down and their hands wander, to take monster slugs of margaritas and then hide behind their sombreros in mock shame—and to record it all in vivid color. Luckily, making a faux photo booth is a snap. Hurr simply hung a colored fabric backdrop, set up her digital camera on a stand, and let her friends click away. The real key is to use a remote control (most newer digital cameras have them) or a cable release (available at photo stores for about $20). Hurr downloaded the images after her party, then sent them to guests as thanks-for-coming notes, though it's easy enough to have the camera hooked up to a computer and printer for instant graphic gratification. It's even possible to lose the computer (and keep it out of booze's way): For about $199, you can get the Olympus P-10 Digital Photo Printer, which connects directly to your digital camera and produces high-quality four-by-six-inch and three-and-a-half-by-five-inch photos in less than a minute. Whatever equipment you choose, you'll want to make certain people get in a goofy groove. Hurr chose a back room— privacy being the key to posing—and provided some choice props, like sombreros, paper flowers, and even her poodle, Baba, who looked a little sheepish but still had the desired stupefying effect on the partygoers. Or was that the tequila?

Fresh guacamole, gringo-style (hold the chiles), above, is a mellow mix made easy when guests pitch in. Opposite: For an affordable authentic touch, get Mexican sodas in flavors like guava, pineapple, even tamarind (about 50 cents a bottle at local Mexican bodegas). You can also order them online for $1.50 each, plus shipping, at MexGrocer.com.

Lettuce Know if You Can Make It

Hurr wanted the invites to set the tone—and table—for this bash. And they did, by asking people to bring specific amounts of fresh ingredients—limes, tomatoes, flour tortillas, etc. Making the invitations is easy: Cut an image out of a supermarket circular and paste it on a card, asking the guest to bring a certain amount of the pictured items. Hurr laid out her design in MS Word, two per 8½-by-11-inch sheet, and printed them on a color inkjet, but the idea works just as well with handwritten notes. The goal here is a potluck party for 12 to 15 that doesn't rely on luck alone, so spell out everything clearly and request the favor of an RSVP, *por favor.* The planning will pay off in your grocery bill (see page 74 for what Hurr asked guests to bring and what she bought herself). You'll find even bigger savings—of your time—if you make food prep a part of the party, right? So just provide an ample supply of cutting boards, bowls, knives (and drinks) to get the guest chefs cooking and chatting—as Jennie Bastian and Hugh Connelly, right, did at Hurr's party while they prepared taco bar fixings and ingredients for Gringo Guacamole.

Lehrmittelverlag

Two dicey dishes for the work of one: Roasted Corn Salsa takes on a new identity with the simple addition of chopped tomatoes.

gemann, Düsseldorf
© 1964 · Printed in Germany 1971

THE RECIPES

roasted corn salsa
(makes about 7½ cups)

- **3 10-oz. bags frozen corn**
- **3 large red bell peppers, diced**
- **3 small finely chopped onions**
- **3–4 cloves garlic, minced**
- **3–4 jalapeño peppers, minced**
- **2–3 limes**
  Salt and pepper
- **6 tomatoes (optional)**

First thing in the morning, place corn in a colander to thaw and let drain until it is completely dry (this can take a while). Then, in a large skillet, roast corn over high heat for about 10 minutes or until it begins to brown. Place corn in a bowl, and add diced peppers and chopped onions. Sprinkle in garlic and jalapeños. Cut up limes and squeeze the juice into mixture. Add salt and pepper to taste.

To make a tomato-corn salsa variation, add 2 to 3 diced tomatoes for each bag of corn you use. Serve with tortilla chips.

gringo guacamole
(makes about 4½ cups)

- **6 avocados**
- **3 tomatoes**
- **1½ finely chopped small onions**
- **1½ cups finely chopped cilantro**
- **3 limes**
  Salt and pepper

Mash avocados in a bowl with a fork, or use a mortar and pestle. Core and seed tomatoes, then dice. Add tomatoes, onions, and cilantro to avocado. Slice and squeeze limes over mixture. Stir until blended. Add salt and pepper to taste.

Tamales to Go-Go

Making tamales, left, is a labor of love best left to pros. So why not pick up fresh ones for about $6 a dozen at your local Mexican restaurant? If you can't find a tamale seller nearby, fear not. Here are two that ship nationally: Alamo Tamales (800-252-0586) and Fat Mama's Tamales (601-442-4548); both charge around $10 a dozen plus shipping—not cheap, but still worth the time it saves. If you order the tamales, you'll likely have to steam them in their husks. Trust us, these tasty treats are like Christmas presents: much more fun to unwrap than to wrap.

Hurr's bright floral platters (a buck each at a local dollar store), above, make the perfect backdrop for ready-made corn taco shells brought by a guest. Left: One thing you can whip up ahead of time is chicken taco filling, a tastier alternative to beef.

chicken taco filling
(serves 15)

3 **whole store-roasted chickens**
3 **7-oz. cans Herdez salsa verde**
Salt and pepper
¾ **cup coarsely chopped cilantro**

Remove chicken from foil bag (important). Peel skin off chicken and shred the meat, pulling it lengthwise into strips. Over a low flame, heat salsa verde in a medium-size saucepan and add chicken to warm it up. Adjust seasoning with salt and pepper. Remove the filling from heat and add cilantro before serving.

Serve with soft flour tortillas (preferably warm) or ready-made corn taco shells, as well as chopped tomatoes and onions, and shredded Monterey Jack cheese and lettuce.

lake michigan margaritas
(makes one 25-oz. pitcher; repeat as necessary)

½ **cup superfine sugar**
1 **cup fresh lime juice**
1 **cup tequila**
1 **tbsp. lime zest**
1 **cup orange juice**

In a pitcher, dissolve superfine sugar in fresh squeezed lime juice. Add tequila. Then, in place of the typical citrus-inflected triple sec, add lime zest and orange juice. Stir and pour over ice (do not add ice to the pitcher; it'll water down your drinks as it melts) or use a drink shaker to strain the cocktail. Note: This sweet libation isn't as sour as traditional margaritas, so salted glasses aren't necessary, if, say, your doctor has prescribed a low-sodium, high-alcohol diet.

THE RECEIPT

YOU BUY

3	10-oz. bags frozen corn	$7.50
2	dozen tamales	$12.00
3	roasted chickens	$21.00
3	7-oz. cans Herdez salsa verde	$4.35
2	dozen tamales	$12.00
1	bunch cilantro	$0.99
1	1.75-1 bottle tequila	$16.00
1	64-oz. carton orange juice	$2.80
24	13.5-oz. bottles Mexican sodas	$12.00
1	ice block	$4.00
1	12-oz. bottle grenadine	$3.49
1	12-oz. bottle Rose's lime juice	$3.49

SUBTOTAL	**$88.87**

GUESTS BRING

3	red bell peppers	$2.97
8	small onions	$1.12
4	jalapeno peppers	$1.69
24	limes	$11.28
12	tomatoes	$6.19
2	14-oz. bags tortilla chips	$3.78
6	ripe avocados	$8.94
2	bunches cilantro	$1.89
2	12-count packages flour tortillas	$1.98
3	12-count packages corn taco shells	$4.47
1	1 lb. Monterey Jack cheese	$4.99
1	head lettuce	$1.49
24	12-oz. bottles Mexican beer	$23.98

SUBTOTAL	**$74.77**
TOTAL	**$163.64**

(tax not included)

ALREADY IN YOUR PANTRY: garlic, salt, and pepper

When the going gets hot, the hot have snow cones. As things warmed up (spicy food, torrid tangos, etc.), Hurr served Mexican-inspired shaved ice—the coolest sweet nothings you can make for next to nothing. She simply scooped the frozen shavings into plastic cups and doused them with either grenadine or sweet lime syrup. To make the syrup, dissolve ½ cup superfine sugar in 1 cup Rose's lime juice.

The final touch: a splash of tequila, perhaps? Admittedly, not everyone has an ice shaver. Electric models cost about $30 at department stores, but nothing beats a hand shaver, like this one from Snoplane (504-885-2050), which runs less than $20. To get authentic block ice, look under ICE DEALERS in the yellow pages; a 25-pound chunk should set you back about $4.

M

Nowhere near Kentucky on race day? You can still throw a bluegrass bash and finish in the money.

Horsing Around

You can take the boy out of Kentucky, but you'll never cure his Derby fever. Or, as Jon Carloftis puts it, "Wherever you are in the world, on the first Saturday in May, something tells you, you'd better be havin' a mint julep and watchin' the race." Born and bred in the Bluegrass State, Carloftis now lives north of the Mason-Dixon Line in Bucks County, Pennsylvania. Still, he has never stopped throwing his annual party to celebrate the run for the roses. And you can bet it's always one stylish soiree. As a sought-after garden designer with clients like Julianne Moore and Edward Norton, Carloftis knows a thing or two about decorating. On race day, he set the stage with a centerpiece of

Guests—including one dressed as a jockey—chomped at the bit before post time, below. Opposite: Bobblehead dolls depicting horse-racing celebs are popular racetrack freebies that often end up on eBay.

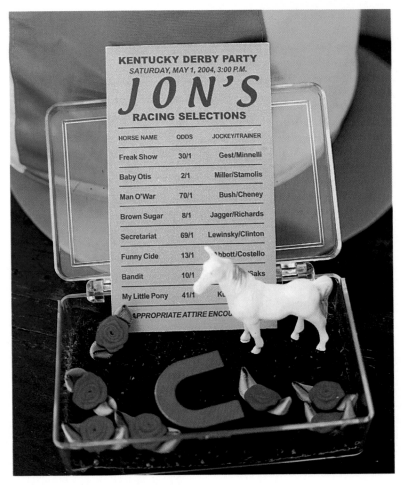

KENTUCKY DERBY PARTY
SATURDAY, MAY 1, 2004, 3:00 P.M.

JON'S
RACING SELECTIONS

HORSE NAME	ODDS	JOCKEY/TRAINER
Freak Show	30/1	Gest/Minnelli
Baby Otis	2/1	Miller/Stamolis
Man O'War	70/1	Bush/Cheney
Brown Sugar	8/1	Jagger/Richards
Secretariat	69/1	Lewinsky/Clinton
Funny Cide	13/1	Abbott/Costello
Bandit	10/1	'Saks
My Little Pony	41/1	K...

APPROPRIATE ATTIRE ENCOU...

Think Inside the Box

Carloftis created his three-dimensional invite by designing a betting ticket on his home computer, then gathering equine-themed tchotchkes like horseshoes and plastic thoroughbreds (both dirt cheap at OrientalTrading.com), plus tiny cloth roses (available at fabric stores) and fake turf scored at Home Depot. He corralled it all inside clear plastic boxes from a dollar store to let folks know they were in for one wild ride.

toy horses grazing on Kentucky bluegrass (okay, Astroturf). He also displayed his commemorative Derby glasses and vintage trading cards and donned a thrift store jacket covered with embroidered horse heads. In a pinch, though, Carloftis insists he can do without all the props. "Good food and drink, plus a mix of people—that's what keeps it interesting," he says.

Over the years Carloftis has perfected a Derby Day menu of traditional dishes he loves because many items (corn pudding, beer cheese, benedictine spread, and even Bibb lettuce salad) can be prepared ahead. Plus, the feast was anchored by a six-pound country ham, which he says "feeds an army for $30." Guests can sip Mint Juleps or guzzle Infield Punch, a vodka concoction known for keeping the rowdy infield crowd at Churchill Downs well lubricated.

On party day, Carloftis woke up early and slipped the ham into the oven. While it cooked, he steamed the asparagus, whipped up the biscuits, built sandwiches, and baked the corn bread. Since all the food could be eaten at room temperature, Carloftis put it out early and started the celebration. By the time guests arrived around 3 P.M., they were greeted with a ready meal, a relaxed host, and a Southern soundtrack that included Alison Krauss, Johnny Cash, and Dolly Parton. With post time hours away, the crowd was free to graze, mingle, and show off their Derby finery.

Minutes before the race, all eyes turned to the TV as Carloftis led a rendition of "My Old Kentucky Home." Then the gates snapped open; for two l*ooo*ng minutes, the party descended into a raucous rebel yell. Moments after the finish, Carloftis rolled back the carpet, bluegrass gave way to Kelis, Ludacris, and Missy Elliot, and for the rest of the night, everyone let fly with moves sure to make a proper Southern lady blush.

Shh, keep it real quiet, but Carloftis, left, has been known to sneak his hip flask into the grandstand. Opposite: One guest saw her fortunes rise, while another, well… Carloftis kept the betting-pool rules simple by ignoring odds; everybody placed a $5 wager and the winner took all.

Yankees who don't cotton to
bourbon can always slurp
vodka-based Infield Punch.

Here's a Hot Tip

The selection of vintage Derby glasses ranges from rare editions that can fetch upwards of $10,000 to cool-looking, if more common, vessels that go for as little as $1 on eBay. The current year's glass is always available at tracks nationwide or online ($9 for two at www.store.yahoo.com/allpro).

Racing Form

What's Derby Day without a silly hat? Scour Grandma's attic or pick one up at a thrift store. You can also have guests create their own by supplying plastic derbies (around $4 a dozen at www.rinovelty.com), glue guns, and the horsey toys used for the party invitation (see page 80).

Revelers jockeyed for position around the TV, left. Above: Carloftis didn't spend big bucks on party decorations; an entire jockey outfit, including cap and goggles, cost about $30 on eBay. Opposite: A $12 junk shop wine coaster displayed an assortment of thoroughbred trading cards from the '30s.

💡 Down-Home Cooking

For a certain breed of Southern woman, recipe trading is a birthright. Carloftis's mother, Lucille, provided the how-to for Beaumont Inn's Corn Pudding, as editor of *Favorite Recipes From a Treasury of Country Inns and Lodges* ($20; www.overmountainpress.com). The recipes for the biscuits, benedictine spread, and beer cheese are compliments of *Bluegrass Winners,* by the Garden Club of Lexington, Kentucky ($20; www.wimmerco.com). Carloftis also recommends *What's Cooking in Kentucky,* by Irene Hayes (out of print; search Google for used copies), and *Out of Kentucky Kitchens,* by Marion Flexner ($25; www.kentuckypress.com).

A True Taste of Kentucky

According to Carloftis, it's not a real Derby party unless you're feasting on country ham. Unlike regular hams, which are sugar-cured for 30 days, the country variety is salt-cured for up to four months. A five to seven pounder ordered from CliftyFarm.com costs $30 plus shipping.

The Recipes

benedictine sandwiches

(serves 15)

- 2 medium cucumbers; 1 peeled and seeded, 1 sliced
- 1 8-oz. package cream cheese, softened
- ½ medium yellow onion, finely grated
  Dash salt
  Dash cayenne pepper
  Green food coloring
- 18 white bread slices, crusts cut off

In a food processor or a blender, grind the peeled cucumber into a pulp, then use cheesecloth to squeeze out juice. Combine pulp with cream cheese, onion, and seasonings, mixing thoroughly. Add a dash of food coloring, just enough to make the spread pale green. Spread mixture between slices of bread, cut into triangles, and top with cucumber slices.

beer cheese and crackers

(serves 15)

- 2 10-oz. blocks extra-sharp cheddar cheese, grated
- 2 cloves garlic, minced
- ¾ cup (6 oz.) beer
- ⅛ tsp. salt
  Tabasco sauce, to taste
  Crackers

In a food processor, combine cheese and garlic, and pulse until combined; add beer and seasonings, and process until thoroughly blended. Transfer to a bowl; refrigerate overnight. Serve with crackers.

country ham

(serves 10)

- 1 5- to 7-lb. uncooked country ham (see caption at left)
- 2 cups brown sugar

Place ham in a bucket and add enough water to cover. Soak ham for at least 2 days in the refrigerator, changing the water twice a day. (Soaking it gets out much of the salt.) Remove ham from water and pat dry. Using your hands, coat ham with a ¼-inch layer of brown sugar. Bake for about 3 hours at 350°F.

beaten biscuits

(makes 6 dozen)

- 7 cups cake flour
- 3 tbsp. sugar

What's Carloftis's philosophy of entertaining? "You're in the home of a Kentuckian; what's mine is yours." Hence, this welcoming buffet, opposite from left: salt-cured country ham; sandwiches made with benedictine spread, a cool mix of cucumber and cream cheese tinted green; Infield Punch, a fruit-juice-and-vodka elixir; and winner's circle–worthy biscuits.

1 tsp. salt
1 tsp. baking powder
1 cup lard
1⅓ cups skim milk

In a large bowl, combine flour, sugar, salt, and baking powder; add lard bit by bit with clean hands. Pour in 1 cup milk, then add remaining milk as needed to make a stiff dough. Refrigerate dough for at least 2 hours. (If the dough has been refrigerated overnight, let it sit at room temperature for 1 hour.) Preheat oven to 350°F. Divide dough into quarters. Working with a quarter at a time, cut dough into 1½-inch cubes, then process cubes in a food processor with a steel blade for 2 minutes. On a floured board, roll out each quarter of dough to ¼-inch thickness; cut with a 2-inch biscuit cutter. Place biscuits on an ungreased cookie sheet; prick the top of each with a fork. Bake for 25 minutes, or until golden.

beaumont inn's corn pudding
(serves 10)
2 cups frozen whole kernel white corn, thawed, or fresh white corn, cut off the cob
8 tbsp. all-purpose flour
1 tsp. salt
4 rounded tsp. sugar
4 tbsp. unsalted butter, melted
4 large eggs
1 qt. whole milk

Preheat oven to 450°F. Mix together corn, flour, salt, sugar, and butter in a large bowl. In a separate bowl, beat eggs well, add milk, then stir into corn mixture. Pour into a large baking dish that's been greased and floured. Bake for 40 to 45 minutes, or until top is golden brown.

cracklin' corn bread
(serves 10)
3–4 tbsp. butter, melted, plus more for greasing
1 cup sifted all-purpose flour
½ tsp. baking soda
1½ tsp. baking powder
1 tbsp. sugar
1 tsp. salt
¾ cup yellow stone-ground cornmeal
1 cup buttermilk
2 large eggs
¼ cup fried bacon, crumbled

Preheat oven to 425°F. Butter a 9-inch-square baking pan and put in the oven. In a large bowl, sift together flour, baking soda, baking powder, sugar, and salt. Stir in cornmeal. In a separate bowl, combine buttermilk, eggs, and butter. Stir wet ingredients into dry. Add bacon. Pour batter into the pan and bake for about 30 minutes.

steamed asparagus
(serves 10)
2 bunches fresh asparagus, stem ends removed
1 lemon
2 tbsp. butter
3 large eggs, hard-boiled

Steam asparagus until bright green, about 4 to 5 minutes.

1.

2.

3.

4.

5.

6.

Booze Clues

Who cares if your horse finishes dead last? "When you're drinking bourbon," Carloftis says, "everybody wins." His six picks:

1. MAKER'S MARK (750 ml; $19) Carloftis calls this 46-year-old brand, famous for its red-wax-sealed bottles, "the premier bourbon. Back in the day, I'd splurge on it to impress a date."

2. WOODFORD RESERVE (750 ml; $25) Another favorite is this supersmooth product of the '90s single-barrel trend. Pricey, but the "beautiful, simple" bottle makes "a great gift."

3. WILD TURKEY 101 (750 ml; $15) "We had Wild Turkey parties in my fraternity," he says. "No mixers." Its 101 proof (most bourbons

are 80 to 90) puts any bash on fast-forward.

4. KNOB CREEK (750 ml; $21) "It has a sweetness that I like," Carloftis says of this small-batch bourbon, bottled at 100 proof as an homage to its pre-Prohibition predecessors.

5. JIM BEAM (750 ml; $11) This well-priced crowd-pleaser is Carloftis's choice for his annual shindig. "If I'm having a bunch of people over," he says, "I'll use this for mixed drinks."

6. EARLY TIMES (750 ml; $8) Not a true bourbon, but this cheap-as-dirt whiskey "gets the job done," Carloftis says—and fuels most of the juleps at Churchill Downs on Derby Day.

Trifecta Pies are a triple threat of bourbon, chocolate chips, and pecans.

Drain and rinse in cold water; pat dry. Place in a serving dish, squeeze lemon juice on top and toss with butter. Garnish with lemon rind and halved hard-boiled eggs.

kentucky bibb lettuce salad
(serves 10)

- 1 lb. green beans, ends removed
- 3 heads Bibb lettuce, torn into large pieces
- 1 package cherry tomatoes
- 1 small red onion, thinly sliced into rings
- 1 8-oz. bottle vinaigrette salad dressing

Steam beans until bright green. Rinse with cold water and pat dry. Place vegetables in a salad bowl, then toss with dressing to taste.

trifecta pie
(serves 8)

- 1 cup plus 6 tbsp. all-purpose flour
- ½ tsp. salt
- ¼ cup vegetable oil
- 2½ tbsp. cold water
- 1 cup sugar
- 1 stick (8 tbsp.) unsalted butter, melted
- 2 large eggs, beaten
- 1 oz. bourbon
- 1 cup coarsely chopped pecans
- 1 cup semisweet chocolate chips

To make crust, mix 1 cup flour and salt in a medium bowl. Pour oil, then water, into dry ingredients; mix. Roll into a ball and refrigerate for 1 hour. Place on wax paper, put another sheet on top, and roll into an 11-inch circle. Pull off the top layer of wax paper and flip dough into a 9-inch metal pie pan. Crimp edges with a fork. Preheat oven to 325ºF. To make filling, combine sugar and remaining flour in a medium bowl. Stir in butter and eggs. Add bourbon, pecans, and chocolate chips. Mix well and pour filling into the pie pan. Bake 50 to 60 minutes or until crust is a pale golden color and filling is set. Cool before serving.

mint juleps
(serves 10)

- ½ cup sugar
- ½ cup warm water
- 2 bunches fresh mint sprigs
- Crushed ice
- 15 oz. Kentucky bourbon

Chill 10 8-oz. silver tumblers in the freezer. Make sugar syrup by combining sugar and warm water and stirring until sugar dissolves. Rub a mint sprig gently along the interior walls of each chilled tumbler—be careful not to crush or mince the leaves. Place crushed ice at the bottom of each tumbler. Pour 1½ tsp. sugar syrup and 1 shot bourbon over ice. Fill tumbler with water to taste. Stir until a frost appears on the outside of the tumbler. Top with a sprig or two of fresh mint.

infield punch
(serves 10)

- 2½ gal. red fruit punch
- 1 750-ml bottle vodka, gin, rum, or pure grain alcohol
- 1 lemon, sliced

Mix punch and liquor in a pitcher. Chill. Just before serving, mix in ice and garnish with lemon slices.

ne

HAVANA PARTY

Kick off summer with a
funky-fresh Latin luau.
The eats and atmosphere are
hot, hot, hot—but they won't
burn through *mucho dinero.*

Miami Heat

Felice Pappas has lived in Miami for 10 years now, but she still sees the sun-drenched city through the eyes of a tourist. Its balmy climate, sorbet-colored buildings, and casual yet flashy dress code continually inspire the Wisconsin native, who creates brightly patterned, pinup-style frocks for her indie clothing company, Love-Life. Her other fashion influences? John Galliano, *Alice in Wonderland*, and Pee Wee Herman. So when Pappas and her boyfriend, Bill Kearney, geared up to throw a summer shindig, it sure wasn't going to be a garden-variety backyard barbecue. Instead, the couple found a theme right under their noses,

THE MENU

tatiana's empadinhas

adobo pork sandwiches

grilled fish tacos with three salsas

black beans and rice

grilled corn on the cob

hearts of palm salad

mini key lime pies

tatiana's brazilian chocolate truffles

ginger-molasses punch with spiced rum

caipiroshkas

strawberry-mint limeade

homemade summer ginger ale

peach-mango lemonade

Pappas scored a set of Carmen Miranda paper dolls on eBay for $14 and gave them a starring role in her invitations, below, which were rolled and sealed with a cigar band. Opposite: Domino sets placed on each table served as an homage to the veteran players in Little Havana's Domino Park.

One guest arrived bearing a local treat—coconut water straight from the source. Pappas chilled the tropical drink in a floral metal tub. The paper cocktail napkins, set in a Cuban cigar box, look so good they oughta be illegal.

Can You Do the Can Can?

There's more than one way to light up the night: Pappas illuminated ethnic food cans, which she bought at Miami bodegas. Use a hammer and awl to perforate the empty tins, string them together with colored electrical wire, then press museum wax inside the cans to secure a tea light in each.

in Miami's own mix of Cuban, South American, and Haitian cultures. "Miami is a melting pot," Pappas says. "I'm lucky that my group of friends reflects that."

Problem was, the bohemian bacchanal that the couple envisioned required room for live music and dancing, and their South Beach pad was a tad tight for 20 guests. Enter good friends Kristen Thiele, a painter, and Frank Casale, a graphic designer, whose delightfully lush backyard in Miami's Little Havana offered the perfect bawdy backdrop. Making the space party-ready wasn't difficult; Thiele and Casale set up card tables swathed in vivid fruit-patterned oilcloths, strung lights through the trees, and moved interior furniture outdoors to create an alfresco living room.

Meanwhile, Pappas took charge of the food. Not willing to abandon her guests for the kitchen, she planned a make-ahead menu of black beans, a pork roast that tastes even better the second day, and tiny key lime pies that require a few hours in the fridge. She also saved time and money by asking guests to bring beer. A foodie pal, Tatiana Silva, donated her prized empadinhas and chocolate truffles. Pappas rounded out the menu with fish tacos and corn on the cob, both cooked on the barbecue, because, as she says, "inevitably one guy will want to prove he's the grill master, so you can pass the tongs and go have a drink." Her beverage selection included limeade and lemonade, as well as vodka-infused Caipiroshkas and a rum-spiked ginger-molasses punch.

It wasn't long before guests let loose to the sounds of Shuttle Lounge and its skewed take on hits by New Order and the Clash. By dusk, tiki torches mellowed the mood; guests savored their nightcaps and enjoyed the warm breezes. Even the hosts were more serene than spent, as if they were on vacation in Brazil or Cuba…or maybe just a cozy backyard in Little Havana.

The hosts (from left, Thiele, Casale, Pappas, and Kearney) took a break around a simple card table draped with a bold $25 oilcloth from Mary Jane Bags (706-866-1741 for stores). Its fruity pattern competed for attention with the gals' lively Love-Life dresses.

Hungry guests lined up—and loaded up—at the buffet, where vivid trays and plates from Crate & Barrel held their own against the colorful fare.

THE RECIPES

tatiana's empadinhas
(makes 36)

- 1½ cups all-purpose flour
- ¼ tsp. salt
- ¼ tsp. baking powder
- 1 stick (8 tbsp.) salted butter, plus 1 tsp., all softened
- 2 eggs, plus 1 egg yolk
- 1 tbsp. cold water
- ⅛ cup milk
- ½ cup shredded Parmesan cheese
- ½ cup shredded mozzarella cheese
- 1 10-oz. package fresh baby spinach, sautéed in olive oil and salt until wilted

Preheat oven to 350°F. Mix dry ingredients, and using your hands, rub in 8 tbsp. butter. Lightly beat together egg yolk and water; add to mixture and combine with your fingers until dough has a smooth texture. Let it rest for 15 minutes at room temperature. In a separate bowl, gently whisk 2 eggs, milk, 1 tsp. butter; add cheeses and spinach, and mix well. Line a mini-muffin-baking pan with muffin cups. Place a small ball of dough in each cup and press flat, then spoon in spinach mixture, almost to the top. Bake about 30 minutes or until golden.

adobo pork sandwiches
(makes 20)

- 2 tbsp. coarse salt
- 2 tbsp. black pepper
- 2 tbsp. dried oregano
- 12 cloves garlic, peeled
- 2 5-lb. boneless pork shoulders
- 6 tbsp. corn oil
- 2 dried bay leaves
- 6 cups chicken or beef stock
- 20 sandwich rolls
- 1¼ lb. Gruyère or Swiss

cheese, sliced
Mayonnaise, for dressing sandwiches

In a food processor, combine salt, pepper, oregano, and garlic, and pulse to form a paste. Spread mixture evenly over pork shoulders and let sit at room temperature for 1 hour. Heat oil in a large stockpot over medium-high heat. Add pork and sear on each side until brown. Add bay leaves and stock, and bring to a boil. Reduce heat to low, cover, and simmer 3 to 4 hours. Remove pork and let cool. Pull meat apart with your hands. Heap shreds of pork onto sandwich rolls dressed with cheese and mayonnaise.

grilled fish tacos
(makes 20)

- 7 tilapia fillets (or any firm white fish)
- 1 10-oz. bottle Badia Mojo (or any orange-based citrus marinade)
- 20 6-inch flour tortillas, warmed in a 250°F oven
  Salsas (see recipes below)
- 1 bunch cilantro, coarsely chopped

Marinate fish in Badia Mojo for 1 hour at room temperature. Place fillets on a hot, lightly oiled grill; cook for 2 to 3 minutes on one side. Flip fish and continue grilling until inside is opaque. Cut each fillet into thirds and serve with warm tortillas, three salsas (see below), and cilantro.

carlos's salsa à la mexicana
(makes 2 cups)

- 10 plum tomatoes, seeded and diced
- 2 medium scallions, chopped (white bulb, plus 2 inches green stalk)

Black beans and rice, top, were served up side by side in a tostada cup. Above: Pappas and her pals worked it to the loony tunes of Shuttle Lounge. Opposite: A trio of salsas—pineapple, cucumber, and one guest's special salsa à la Mexicana—amped up the flavor of grilled fish tacos.

4 Serrano chiles, seeded and minced
1 cup cilantro, chopped
4 tbsp. lime juice
2 tsp. salt

Combine ingredients in a bowl and refrigerate 2 to 3 hours. Add salt just before serving.

pineapple salsa
(makes 2 cups)

1 pineapple, peeled, cored, and cut into ¼-inch cubes
1 bunch scallions, chopped (white bulb, plus 2 inches green stalk)
2 tbsp. ginger, peeled and grated
2 tbsp. fresh lime juice

Combine ingredients in a bowl; refrigerate 2 to 3 hours before serving.

cucumber salsa
(makes 3 cups)

4 cucumbers, peeled, seeded, and cut into ¼-inch pieces
2 orange bell peppers, seeded and cut into ¼-inch pieces
1 cup chopped cilantro
1 tsp. sugar
½ cup rice wine vinegar
Salt, to taste

Combine cucumbers, peppers, and cilantro. In a separate bowl, dissolve sugar in vinegar; toss with vegetables and refrigerate 2 to 3 hours. Add salt just before serving.

black beans and rice
(makes 20)

1½ lb. dry black beans
10–12 cups cold water
6 tbsp. olive oil
3 small yellow onions, chopped
3 small green bell peppers, chopped
6 cloves garlic, minced
3 tsp. dried oregano
3 packets Sazón Goya (without Annatto)
6 tbsp. cider vinegar
3 tsp. salt

¾ tsp. ground black pepper
3 14-oz. boxes instant white rice
20 corn tostada cups
1 small bunch cilantro, coarsely chopped

In a large pot, combine beans with cold water and let stand overnight at room temperature. Drain and rinse beans. Pour 12 cups fresh water over beans and let stand; do not drain. Meanwhile, heat oil in a skillet over medium heat and sauté onions, peppers, and garlic until tender, about 5 minutes. Add oregano, Sazón Goya, vinegar, salt, and ground pepper to skillet; mix thoroughly. Remove from heat, put mixture in pot with beans, and bring to a boil. Reduce heat, cover, and simmer until beans are tender, about 45 minutes. Prepare rice according to package directions. Fill one side of each tostada cup with rice, the other with beans. Garnish with cilantro. (You may be able to buy premade tostada cups, so check with your local Mexican restaurant. Or you can make your own using nonstick bowl bakers—$10 for two at KitchenCollection.com.)

grilled corn on the cob
(makes 20)

20 ears sweet corn, with husks on
Salt, to taste
Paprika, to taste
Butter, to taste

Carefully pull husks away from corncobs without detaching the leaves from the stems. Remove as much of the corn silk as possible and re-cover corn with husks. Place corn directly on

a medium-low grill and cook, with the lid closed, for 15 to 20 minutes, turning ears every 5 minutes. To see if they're done, peel away part of a husk and check for tenderness. When tender, dehusk corn and place it on the grill for another 5 minutes, lid off, to char. Remove from heat and season with salt, paprika, and butter.

hearts of palm salad
(serves 20)

4 14-oz. cans hearts of palm, drained, rinsed, and thinly sliced
4 red bell peppers, cored and thinly sliced
4 yellow bell peppers, cored and thinly sliced
4 jalapeño peppers, seeded and thinly sliced
2 medium red onions, peeled and thinly sliced
4 cloves garlic, peeled and thinly sliced
1 bunch cilantro, chopped
1 cup extra virgin olive oil
4 limes, juiced
4 tsp. salt
1½ tsp. freshly ground black pepper
2 pineapples, peeled, cored, and sliced into strips

Combine hearts of palm, peppers, onions, garlic, and cilantro, and toss. In another bowl, whisk oil slowly into lime juice, salt, and black pepper. Pour over vegetables and toss again to coat. Fold pineapple into salad.

mini key lime pies
(makes 20)

10 egg yolks
2 14-oz. cans sweetened condensed milk
1⅓ cups bottled key lime juice
½ tbsp. vanilla
20 Keebler graham cracker mini piecrusts
4 limes, thinly cut into 20 slices

Go All Out

It's okay to relocate living room furniture to the great outdoors—for one afternoon. A tufted thrift store sofa, Pier One's rattan saucer chairs, and an Oriental rug from Overstock.com transformed the backyard into an opulent open-air parlor.

A pitcher of Caipiroshkas, right foreground, offered a Russian take on the classic Brazilian caipirinha by swapping out cachaca, a hard-to-find sugarcane liquor, in favor of good ol' vodka. It led a pack of punches flavored with kiwi, mangoes, strawberries, peaches, ginger, mint, and rosemary.

Preheat oven to 350°F. Using an electric mixer, beat yolks, then add condensed milk, juice, and vanilla; continue whipping until consistency is smooth. Fill each piecrust almost to the top with custard and bake for 10 minutes, until firm. Chill up to 48 hours. Garnish with lime slice.

tatiana's brazilian chocolate truffles
(makes 32)

- **1 tbsp. salted butter, plus more for forming truffles**
- **1 14-oz. can sweetened condensed milk**
- **3 tbsp. Nestlé Nesquik chocolate powdered drink mix**
- **1 cup chocolate sprinkles**

Melt butter in a saucepan, and blend in condensed milk and chocolate powder. Simmer on low, stirring constantly to prevent milk from burning. Continue cooking until mixture has consistency of melted caramel—about 20 minutes. Transfer to a glass bowl and refrigerate for 1 hour, or until mixture has the consistency of Play-Doh. Coat your palms with butter and roll mixture into ½-inch balls. Roll them in chocolate sprinkles, pressing hard until each ball is covered.

ginger-molasses punch with spiced rum
(makes 12 cups)

- **4 tbsp. Bacardi light rum**
- **1 6-inch knob ginger, scrubbed and cut into thin slices**
- **2 cups molasses**
- **2 tbsp. freshly squeezed lime juice**
- **2 cups Castillo spiced rum Lime slices**

In a large pot, bring 12 cups water, light rum, ginger, molasses, and lime juice to a boil. Reduce heat and simmer uncovered for 20 minutes. Remove from heat and let cool. Strain liquid and refrigerate for several hours until cold. In a 1-gal. container, mix in spiced rum. Serve over ice and garnish with lime slices.

caipiroshkas
(makes 16 cups)

- **2 cups sugar**
- **6 cups freshly squeezed lime juice**
- **5 cups vodka Lime slices**

In a saucepan, bring sugar and 4 cups water to a boil. Simmer until sugar has dissolved, stirring occasionally, about 6 to 8 minutes. Remove from heat and refrigerate until cool. In a 1-gal. container, mix syrup with lime juice and vodka. Serve over ice and garnish with lime slices.

strawberry-mint limeade
(makes 16 cups)

- **10 kiwis**
- **2 lb. strawberries**
- **4 cups cold water**
- **2 cups Mint Simple Syrup (see recipe on page 102)**
- **2 cups freshly squeezed lime juice**

Peel kiwis and remove leaves from strawberries. Reserve half a kiwi and 4 strawberries for garnish. Puree remaining fruit in a food processor and strain through a sieve. In a 1-gal. container, combine water, Mint Simple Syrup, fruit puree, and lime juice. Serve over ice and garnish with thin slices of kiwi and strawberry halves.

homemade summer ginger ale
(makes 16 cups)

- **4 cups Ginger Simple Syrup (see recipe on page 102)**
- **12 cups club soda**
- **½ pt. fresh blueberries**

In 1-gal. container, just before serving, mix the Ginger Simple Syrup and club soda. Serve immediately over ice and garnish with blueberries.

peach-mango lemonade

(makes 16 cups)

- 8 fresh mangoes, peeled and cut into chunks
- 12 fresh peaches, cut into chunks
- 6 cups cold water
- 4 cups Rosemary Simple Syrup (see recipe below)
- 2 cups freshly squeezed lemon juice
- Few sprigs rosemary

Using food processor, puree fruit and strain through a sieve. In a 1-gal. container, combine fruit puree with water, Rosemary Simple Syrup, and lemon juice. Serve over ice and garnish with rosemary.

infused simple syrups

(makes 2 cups mint, 4 cups ginger and rosemary)
For mint syrup:

- 1⅛ cups sugar
- 2¼ cups water
- 1 bunch fresh mint leaves, washed

For ginger syrup:

- 2¼ cups sugar
- 4½ cups water
- 1 6-inch knob ginger, scrubbed and thinly sliced

For rosemary syrup:

- 2¼ cups sugar
- 4½ cups water
- 2 bunches rosemary, washed

For each syrup, bring sugar and water to a boil, stirring until sugar dissolves. Reduce heat to low, add mint, ginger, or rosemary, and simmer syrup and herbs for 2 minutes. Remove from heat and let steep for 15 minutes. Strain. The syrups can be refrigerated in an airtight container for up to 2 weeks.

Guests couldn't resist the tang of Mini Key Lime Pies, below. Opposite: As the party wound down, Kearney sidled up to Pappas and counted the empties before last call.

A Fourth with no flags? Or franks on the grill? Declare your independence and throw a birthday party to make Uncle Sam proud.

Guests headed to the deck, left, to watch the rockets' red glare (okay, fireworks) at the twilight's last gleaming. Opposite: Fresh raspberries, lemons, and blueberries flavored patriotically colored Popsicles.

Red, White, and New

When Alexandra and Eliot Angle decided to host a Fourth of July fete at their pad in Los Angeles's Echo Park, they knew they wanted a cookout by the pool with a dozen or so friends. But they weren't up for the traditional trappings of Independence Day. Not that they have anything against sparklers, Stars and Stripes bunting, or John Philip Sousa, it's just that the Angles, who started the interior design and event-planning firm Aqua Vitae Design, are always careful to match the party to the house. And one look at their wide casement windows, sparse furniture, cinder block walls, and bamboo grove will tell you that simple decoration was in order.

So while the Angles skipped elaborate homages to Old Glory for this chic celebration, they did use the patriotic palette's three colors—albeit in completely unexpected ways. Chinese paper lanterns hung at varying heights delivered Asian simplicity, as well as huge hits of red, white, and blue. The flag's hues also appeared in the illuminated wine bottles that lined the pool perimeter and buffet table. And bright red carnations in mismatched blue-and-white teacups and vases evoked Independence Day without pledging allegiance to propaganda.

In true Angle fashion, the party food was as sophisticated but unfussy as the decor. The pair's one guiding principle? Freshness—pure and simple. "We really believe in using seasonal ingredients for drinks and recipes," Alexandra says. "We focus on less and try to perfect it." For this get-together, that meant summery fruits and vegetables all around. In between bites of savory ginger-and-soy-marinated grilled chicken, guests sampled jicama salad with cherry tomatoes and fresh mint, shrimp ceviche served in cups carved out of cucumbers, and a frozen cocktail called a Ruby Slip, which the Angles created from vodka, raspberries, and peaches. Instead of simply doctoring some Duncan Hines cupcakes, Alexandra made a batch from scratch—using red-white-and-blue-frosted stars and

All grown-up doesn't always require getting all dressed up, above. Alexandra (far left) and Eliot Angle (center, in the green T-shirt) let freedom ring and flip-flops reign at their informal fete.

Show Your Colors

Red, white, and blue doesn't have to mean miniature flags. The Angles gave the hues a more sophisticated twist by setting out $3-a-bunch carnations (yes, the much belittled bloom is good for more than boutonnieres) in a variety of flea market–bought blue-and-white china. Vases work, but so do teacups, teapots, and custard cups—the more varied the size and shape, the better. Can't stand carnies? Splurge on red and white roses, peonies, or gerberas.

Let There Be Light

Instead of tossing those empty wine bottles in the trash bin, why not recycle them yourself? The Angles, with their signature touch (no Chianti bottles turned candlesticks here), filled theirs with water and added red or blue food dye, or, for a white tint, a few drops of milk. Then they placed tea lights behind the bottles to give the occasion some affordable ambience.

Alexandra, below, sorted through Chinese lanterns (available at PearlRiver.com) in the day's colors. Opposite: Guests soaked up the warm glow of the bright lights.

peace signs for decoration. Even the Patriotic Popsicles, which could have easily gone the food-coloring route, got their hues from blueberries, raspberries, and lemons—not a time-consuming project, but one best prepared for.

Amidst all their planning, the couple also planned on the unexpected, leaving a handful of the final unfinished chores for guests to do. "It makes them feel comfortable, like it's their party—which it is," Alexandra says. So when a few invitees showed up before the table was set or the drinks mixed, they were put to work. "It helped us out," she says, "and made them less embarrassed about being the first people to arrive."

When a new wave of friends rolled in, the hosts directed everybody down to the patio and pool. "It's cozy down there, which gets everybody mingling," Eliot says. While some of the guests changed into bathing suits and splashed about, others nibbled and sipped Ruby Slips or Bud longnecks, which were kept on ice in a birdbath.

By the time the sun (and the food and more than a few drinks) had gone down, the guests had all made their way upstairs to the Angles' deck to take in to-die-for views of the Hollywood Hills, the Pacific Ocean, and—once a year—the fireworks over Dodger Stadium. Now, what could possibly be more American than that?

THE RECIPES

ceviche cucumber cups
(serves 12)

- **1–1¼ lb. small shrimp, peeled and deveined**
- **½ cup lime juice**
- **½ cup finely chopped white onion**
- **⅓ cup chopped fresh cilantro**
- **⅓ cup tomato sauce**
- **1 tbsp. superfine sugar**
- **2 tbsp. Mexican hot sauce (look for a brand listing vinegar as the first ingredient)**
- **2 tbsp. extra virgin olive oil**
- **1 small ripe avocado, peeled, pitted, and chopped into small cubes**
- **Salt, for seasoning**
- **4 hothouse cucumbers**

Bring 1 qt. salted water to boil. Chop shrimp into small pieces and add to water. When shrimp is uniformly pink, strain and set aside in a large bowl. In a separate bowl, combine lime juice, onion, cilantro, tomato sauce, sugar, hot sauce, and olive oil, and pour over shrimp. Add avocado and stir to combine. Cover and refrigerate for 1 to 2 hours. When ready to serve, season with salt.

To make cups, peel cucumbers and cut into chunks an inch or so thick. Using a melon baller or a small spoon, scoop out the center of each chunk.

Fill each cup with ceviche and serve.

jicama, tomato, and corn salad
(serves 12)

- **1 large jicama (or 4 cucumbers)**
- **3 pt. cherry tomatoes**
- **3 ears fresh corn**
- **¼ cup fresh mint leaves**
- **1 oz. tequila**
- **2 tbsp. lime juice**
- **2 tbsp. lemon juice**
- **10 tbsp. canola oil**
- **Salt and pepper, to taste**

Peel jicama and slice into ice-cube-size chunks. Halve cherry tomatoes. Lightly steam corn for about 5 minutes. When done, run cobs under cold water and slice off the kernels using a sharp knife. Mix jicama, tomatoes, and corn kernels in a large bowl. For dressing, combine mint, tequila, lime juice, lemon juice, and oil in a blender, and puree. Add salt and pepper to taste. Dress salad just before serving.

ginger-soy chicken skewers
(serves 12)

- **4½ lb. boneless, skinless chicken breast**
- **1 cup soy sauce**
- **¾ cup white wine**
- **⅓ cup sugar**
- **4 tbsp. grated fresh ginger**
- **1 tbsp. salt**

Guests sipped Ruby Slips, top left. Bottom left: Cucumber cups held individual servings of shrimp ceviche. Opposite: Dinner consisted of grilled ginger-soy chicken skewers and a salad of jicama, summer tomatoes, and corn.

Bottoms Up

What's more patriotic than serving good old-fashioned American Bud? And what's more unexpected than chilling it in a birdbath? The Angles tucked longnecks into an ice-filled basin, above, that's perfectly perched on a trio of tree limbs in their backyard.

4 tbsp. canola oil
4 tbsp. sesame oil
2 8-oz. cans whole water chestnuts
 Skewers (if wooden, soak in water overnight before using)

Cut chicken into 1-inch cubes. Combine all other ingredients except water chestnuts in a large bowl. Add chicken and toss to coat completely. Cover and refrigerate for at least 1 hour to marinate. Assemble skewers by alternating between pieces of chicken and water chestnuts (go slowly; these guys are delicate). Grill over a medium-high flame for about 5 minutes a side or until chicken is opaque throughout.

patriotic popsicles
(makes 12)

1¼ cups sugar
1½ cups raspberries or strawberries
1¼ cups lemon juice
1½ cups blueberries
½ lime, juiced
 Popsicle containers or small paper cups
 Popsicle sticks

Combine 2 cups water and sugar in a pot. Place over medium heat until sugar has dissolved. Remove from heat and let cool.

To make red stripe: Puree raspberries and strain to remove seeds. Combine with ¾ cup lemon juice and ⅔ cup sugar water. Distribute evenly among Popsicle containers and freeze until set, about 2 hours.

To make white stripe: Add ½ cup lemon juice to ⅔ cup sugar water. Distribute evenly over raspberry layer. Freeze until set.

To make blue stripe: Puree blueberries in a food processor. Strain through a sieve over a bowl to remove seeds and skin, pushing mixture through the wires with a rubber spatula, if necessary. Mix blueberry juice with lime juice and the rest of the sugar water. Pour over lemon layer, insert Popsicle sticks, and put in the freezer until solid.

chocolate cupcakes
(makes 12)

Cupcake
4 oz. unsweetened chocolate
1¼ cups milk
1 cup light brown sugar, firmly packed
3 egg yolks
½ cup sweet butter, softened
1 cup white sugar
1 tsp. vanilla extract
1¾ cups cake flour
1 tsp. baking soda
1 tsp. salt
2 egg whites

Icing
8 oz. cream cheese, softened
1 tbsp. corn syrup
1 cup confectioners' sugar, sifted
1 tsp. vanilla extract

The Angles' most intoxicating invention, the Ruby Slip, middle. Near: The red, white, and blue decor was the icing on the cake—or at least the homemade chocolate cupcakes.

1 tbsp. grated orange rind
Red and blue decorator's icing (available at supermarkets)

Preheat oven to 375°F. Line muffin tins with paper baking cups.

In the top of a double boiler, over boiling water, heat chocolate, ½ cup milk, brown sugar, and 1 egg yolk. Whisk continuously and, when smooth and thick, remove from heat. In a large bowl, cream together butter and sugar. Add the remaining 2 egg yolks, ¾ cup milk, and vanilla, and beat until smooth. In a separate bowl, sift together flour, baking soda, and salt. Slowly add to sugar and butter mixture, and beat until smooth. Pour in chocolate mixture and combine. In a nonreactive (read: not metal) bowl, beat egg whites until stiff and fold gently into batter. Pour batter into muffin tins and bake for 20 to 25 minutes. Remove from oven and let rest for 10 minutes in tins. Then remove from tins and let cool completely on a wire rack.

Mix together cream cheese, corn syrup, confectioners' sugar, vanilla, and orange rind in a bowl, and use to frost cupcakes once they are cool. Embellish with red and blue decorator's icing as desired.

ruby slip
(makes 1)

2 oz. vodka
½ oz. limoncello*
⅓ cup raspberries
½ fresh peach
½ cup ice
  * If you can't find limoncello, use a mixture of equal parts simple syrup and lemon juice.

Combine all ingredients in a blender and blend until smooth. Serve in a martini glass.

THE RECEIPT

1.5 lb. fresh shrimp		$11.24
6 limes		$2.82
1 white onion		$0.99
2 bunches fresh cilantro		$1.78
1 8-oz. can tomato sauce		$0.49
1 16-oz. box superfine sugar		$1.09
1 6-oz. bottle Mexican hot sauce		$0.79
1 small avocado		$0.79
4 hothouse cucumbers		$7.72
1 large jicama		$1.13
3 pt. cherry tomatoes		$5.85
3 ears corn		$1.49
1 bunch fresh mint		$1.99
1 32-oz. bottle lemon juice		$2.19
4.5 lb. boneless, skinless chicken breast		$23.79
1 10-oz. bottle soy sauce		$1.69
1 750-ml bottle white wine		$4.99
1 4-lb. bag granulated sugar		$2.29
1/4 lb. ginger		$0.99
1 6-oz. bottle sesame oil		$2.19
2 8-oz. cans whole water chestnuts		$1.38
1 100-count box 9-inch bamboo skewers		$1.79
2 1/2-pt. raspberries		$5.00
2 1/2-pt. blueberries		$5.00
1 50-count box paper cups		$2.49
1 50-count box Freezer Pop sticks		$2.00
1 4-oz. package unsweetened chocolate		$2.59
1 16-oz. box light brown sugar		$0.89
6 eggs		$0.95
1 8-oz. tub sweet butter		$3.49
1 2-lb. bag cake flour		$1.95
1 8-oz. package cream cheese		$1.19
1 1-lb. box confectioners' sugar		$0.89
1 orange		$0.29
1 0.68-oz. tube red decorator's icing		$1.75
1 0.68-oz. tube blue decorator's icing		$1.75
1 750-ml bottle vodka		$7.69
1 750-ml bottle limoncello		$20.99
6 peaches		$1.20
2 18-packs Budweiser		$23.98
TOTAL		**$163.56**
(tax not included)		

ALREADY IN YOUR PANTRY: olive oil, salt, tequila, canola oil, pepper, milk, vanilla, baking soda, corn syrup

Organic "fast food" and a backyard slumber party make for a swell summer soiree under the stars.

HIGH CAMP

Say the words "organic food" and most folks picture tasteless tidbits of tofu or a single head of lettuce sporting a six-dollar price tag. Whatever comes to mind, though, chances are, it doesn't involve beers and burgers, s'mores and slasher flicks, all served up at an outdoor end-of-summer bash that rages all night long. Of course, the hosts behind this particular campy campout aren't your typical environmental activists. Brian Benavidez and Melissa Locker opened Sparky's American Food in Brooklyn, New York, to create cuisine that's earth- *and* people-friendly. So while the couple insist on free-range beef and locally grown, pesticide-free produce, they spin the rarefied raw materials into affordable feel-good fare—think humble hamburgers, hot dogs, and french fries.

THE MENU

deviled eggs

hamburgers, hot dogs, and tofu dogs

fire-roasted vegetable toppings

chipotle-coated corn

coleslaw

tomato salad

s'mores

lemonade iced tea

pabst blue ribbon and brooklyn lager beer

cranberry-nut oatmeal

coffee

Cuddly campers—tucked into
Coleman's classic flannel-lined
sleeping bags (about $22 each)—
played footsie under the covers.

Of all the down-home chow on their party menu, Brian Benavidez and Melissa Locker found frankfurters (beef for him, tofu for her) easiest to prep: Skewer, roast over the fire, and eat. Best of all, each guest did his or her own cooking, leaving the happy hosts time to kick back and share a laugh.

Even better are the celebrated restaurant's prices: Where else can you get a hearty organic meal for $3 to $7? "The movement is really expensive," Benavidez admits, "and that's what we're trying to change. We want to bring it down to earth."

In this case, literally. On a summer Saturday, the duo rounded up a motley crew and got back to the land—albeit the lush, neatly mowed land behind a friend's house in upstate New York, where they staged an adult take on the open-air sleepover. Like the seemingly contradictory idea of organic "fast food," a backyard campout combines the best of both worlds—the style and ease of an indoor event (a stove and toilet just a few yards away!) with the palpably magical experience of sleeping and eating under the stars. And what better way to celebrate summer's last gasp than with a recap of the season's greatest highlights—the cookout, the woodsy hike, even the drive-in (really just a TV and VCR dragged outside for an evening screening of *Friday the 13th*)? Benavidez and Locker managed to pack it all into their 24-hour shindig, in part because they kept the menu simple and straightforward.

In addition to burgers and hot dogs (plus a few tofu franks for vegetarian pals), the couple whipped up warm-weather classics like deviled eggs, tomato salad,

(Cool) Campfire Songs

Sing-alongs around the flames can be pretty sappy—unless you plot a playlist that's a little bit country and a little bit rock 'n' roll, like Locker did. Want great reception at your campout? Splurge on Coleman's Cool Box (an ice chest, CD player, and radio in one for around $200). Here, it was stocked with a high-low mix of Pabst Blue Ribbon and Brooklyn Lager, courtesy of the guests.

Johnny Cash
AMERICAN RECORDINGS

20th Century Masters
THE BEST OF HANK WILLIAMS

The Modern Lovers
THE MODERN LOVERS

Calexico
SPOKE

Bruce Springsteen
NEBRASKA

Tom Waits
SWORDFISHTROMBONES

Run-D.M.C.
GREATEST HITS

Har Mar Superstar
HAR MAR SUPERSTAR

Lucinda Williams
CAR WHEELS ON A GRAVEL ROAD

The Magnetic Fields
69 LOVE SONGS, VOLUME 3

Pinback
BLUE SCREEN LIFE

Holly Golightly
THE MAIN ATTRACTION

Fright Night

You don't need to spend big to achieve a little drive-in–worthy drama in the backyard, opposite. Instead of a pricey projector rental, simply link up a few extension cords and roll your TV and DVD player (or VCR) onto the lawn. For thrill seekers, Benavidez and Locker recommend *The Blair Witch Project*, *The Shining*, and, of course, *Friday the 13th*. Want more noogies than white knuckles? Both *Meatballs* and *Wet Hot American Summer* get two thumbs-up.

and s'mores, then paired them with new takes on old summertime standards. The coleslaw, for instance, derived its maroon hue from shredded brilliant red cabbage. The roasted corn was served smothered in smoky chipotle butter and grated Parmesan. Instead of plain old ketchup, mustard, or mayo, guests topped their burgers and dogs with grilled farm-fresh tomatoes and roasted onions and garlic.

The only embargoed items around the campfire were wasteful paper products. Why use downscale disposable dishware when affordable, eco-conscious, and stylish options abound? Steel plates that cost only $2.50 apiece, vintage tumblers borrowed from the kitchen, and napkins cut from funky old fabric scraps helped establish the campout's nostalgic tone, while also making it clear that this was a distinctly grown-up gathering. And, as the guests could attest, the experience only got better with age: You could eat dessert first, share a tent with whomever you chose, stay up till dawn, then gulp a cup of coffee with your oatmeal.

That, after all, is the point—of the couple's party and their restaurant. It's about getting back to a simpler, sweeter way of life, sans the sanctimonious rules. As Benavidez explains, "Our mission with Sparky's is serious. It's about supporting family farming and providing pure, tasty food. It can be hard, but we don't want our customers to worry about all that. We just want them to be happy and to enjoy themselves." Doing good while having a good time. How could they not?

An equal mix of nurture and nature made for happy campers. The gang, top left, took a midday walk through the woods behind the house. Middle left: A slew of steel flashlights proved handy for late-night hikes—and horror stories. Bottom left: Your aim may be true, but if the truth is incriminating, this truth-or-dare dartboard ensures you'll get raked over the coals long after the last burger has been flipped.

Guests loaded up their old-school steel sectional plates with summer classics like coleslaw and grilled corn.

MERIT BADGE NOT REQUIRED

You don't need to be a pelt-wearing outdoorsman to plan a killer campout. The smallest spark of ingenuity—when it comes to such defining details as invitations, favors, lighting, and napkins—is all it takes to ensure your party is a blazing success.

MAIL CALL Locker crafted her own invitations, above right, from origami paper, gift wrap, and brown grocery bags. For favors, she and Benavidez filled $1 flashlights from a local five-and-dime with goodies (and batteries). Oriental Trading.com is a great source for cheap, kitschy trinkets—12 frog key chains cost $4—while Coleman.com carries affordable outdoorsy accessories, like these waterproof matches. For silly sweets, check out DiscountCandy.com, where the Sparky's crew stocks up on hot dog and hamburger gummis.

GET LIT Lightning bugs can only do so much. Entertaining without electricity requires an extra charge of inspiration. Benavidez and Locker found mason jars for less than a buck each at Polsteins.com and rigged them as hurricane lamps, right.

GOOD CLEAN (GREEN) FUN When linens are too fussy, but Bounty seems more redneck than rustic (not to mention wasteful), take a pair of pinking shears to some fabric scraps and create relaxed—and completely reusable—napkins with a decorative edge, below right.

Open your ears: Corn grilled with the husks on, above, was ready for shucking and eating. Opposite left: Deviled eggs sat steady on a Crate & Barrel plate made especially for them. Opposite right: Who knew that three simple ingredients—in this case, chocolate, marshmallows, and graham crackers—could reduce adults to giddy, drooling children? To tempt 10 people with warm, gooey s'mores you'll need three 7-ounce bars of milk chocolate, one 16-ounce box of graham crackers, and one 10-ounce bag of marshmallows.

THE RECIPES

deviled eggs
(makes 24)

- 1 dozen hard-boiled eggs
- ¼ cup plus 2 tbsp. mayonnaise
- 2 tbsp. Dijon mustard
- 1 tsp. Worcestershire sauce
- 1 tbsp. cider vinegar
- ½ tsp. salt
- ½ tsp. pepper
  Paprika, for garnish

Peel eggs and half lengthwise. Carefully scoop out yolks. Put reserved yolks in a medium bowl and place whites on a serving platter. With a fork, mash yolks, and add mayo, mustard, Worcestershire, vinegar, salt, and pepper. Mix until smooth and fluffy. Spoon yolk mixture into whites and top each with paprika.

hot dogs, tofu dogs, and hamburgers
(serves 10)

- 1 8-link package free-range beef hot dogs
- 1 8-link package tofu dogs
- 3 lb. free-range hamburger meat
- 2 tbsp. finely chopped cilantro
- 3 tsp. chipotle powder (or to taste)
- 2 tsp. coarse salt
- 4 tbsp. melted butter
- 1 12-count package hamburger buns
- 1 12-count package hot dog buns
- 1 head green leaf lettuce, shredded
  Fire-Roasted Vegetable Toppings (see below right)

Skewer beef and tofu dogs on long sticks. For beef franks, roast over campfire for about 4 minutes, or until they darken. For tofu, look for grill-specific varieties (made without casings) and follow package directions. For burgers, you'll either need to rig a grate atop the fire or, as Benavidez and Locker did, rely on a nearby backyard grill. To prepare meat, place it in a large bowl; sprinkle in cilantro, chipotle powder, and salt, and mix well. Form into 10 patties. Grill over high heat, turning occasionally and brushing with melted butter. Cook to your liking (a medium burger takes about 10 minutes and is firm to the touch) or until a meat thermometer inserted in the middle reads 165°F. Serve burgers and dogs with buns, lettuce, and vegetable toppings.

fire-roasted vegetable toppings
(serves 10)

- 2 yellow onions
- 2 heads garlic

Olive oil, to coat
4 tomatoes

Trim heads off onions and garlic, and peel away papery outer layers. Slice onions. Coat onions and garlic in olive oil, and wrap in individual foil packets. Throw on the fire or grill over medium-high heat for about 30 minutes or until tender. Slice tomatoes and brush with olive oil. Because tomatoes are delicate, they must be cooked atop a grill (either a grate placed over the fire or a backyard charcoal grill) over medium-high heat until tender and somewhat blackened. Let guests top each burger and dog with onion and tomato. Squeeze garlic from bulb and mash atop meat.

chipotle-coated corn

(serves 10)

10 ears corn, in the husk
1 tbsp. olive oil
2 tbsp. chopped red onion
3 tbsp. chipotle powder
2 sticks (16 tbsp.) unsalted butter, softened
Salt and pepper
2 limes
1 cup grated Parmesan

Grill corn over medium heat for about 15 to 20 minutes, turning often, until husks are lightly blackened. While corn is roasting, retreat to the kitchen stove and heat olive oil in a small saucepan. Sauté onion in oil until soft and translucent. Add 1 tsp. chipotle powder and cook another minute. Remove pan from heat and let cool. Add butter and blend until smooth. Season with salt and pepper. Slice lime into wedges. Remove husk from corn, coat ear in butter mixture, and cover with cheese. Dust with additional chipotle powder and squirt with a lime wedge prior to serving.

coleslaw

(serves 10)

1 cup mayonnaise
6 tbsp. cider vinegar
⅓ cup barbecue sauce
3 tbsp. sugar
½ tsp. cayenne pepper (or to taste)
12 cups shredded red cabbage (about 2 heads)
Salt and pepper, to taste

Mix mayo, vinegar, barbecue sauce, sugar, and cayenne in a large bowl. Add cabbage to mixture. Toss to coat and season with salt and pepper.

tomato salad

(serves 10)

8 ripe but firm large tomatoes
5 tbsp. olive oil
5 tbsp. cider vinegar
3 tsp. dried oregano
1½ tsp. salt, plus more to taste
Pepper, to taste

1.

2.

3.

4.

COFFEE TALK

Can't afford premium Viennese or Costa Rican java but refuse to dwell in the house of Maxwell? Several less expected budget blends will pass through your filter with flying colors. Here, four roasts that are truly good to the last drop.

1. CAFÉ BUSTELO Sure, the packaging rocks. But that's not all. This high-octane, intensely aromatic Latin import is as bold as the can that holds it. It's a surefire way to start your day at full throttle. (www.coffeecabana.com, $3 for 10 ounces)

2. EIGHT O'CLOCK COFFEE Ease into the A.M. with this smooth, well-blended taster's choice. You'll need a grinder, since whole beans are the key to this brand's fresh flavor. (800-299-2739 for locations, $4 for 13 ounces)

3. COMMUNITY COFFEE This Baton Rouge, Louisiana–based company offers a New Orleans blend that's pleasantly earthy with a hint of chicory. Think of it as a poor man's Cafe du Monde. (www.communitycoffee.com, $5 for 16 ounces)

4. CAFE PILON Big flavor and lots of caffeine make this Cuban staple *muy bueno* for café con leche. Budget bonus: It's so strong that you can skimp on the grinds and still get a good buzz going. (www.coffeecabana.com, $3 for 10 ounces)

Wash, core, and cut each tomato into 8 wedges. In a medium bowl, whisk together olive oil and vinegar. Add tomatoes, stir to coat, and sprinkle with oregano and salt. Cover and chill for at least 2 hours or overnight. Season with extra salt and pepper.

lemonade iced tea
(serves 10)

    7 **bags Darjeeling tea**
1½ **cups sugar**
    4 **sprigs fresh mint, plus more if desired**

As for the morning after…you don't have to toil over some big trucker breakfast to send overnight guests home well fed. Benavidez and Locker kept it simple by serving hot coffee and spooning out creamy oatmeal topped with cranberry and nuts.

THE RECEIPT

1	dozen eggs	$1.39
1	16-oz. jar mayonnaise	$1.69
1	8-link package free-range hot dogs	$3.99
1	8-link package tofu dogs	$2.39
3	lb. free-range hamburger meat	$11.97
1	bunch fresh cilantro	$1.99
1	3-oz. jar chipotle powder	$4.95
4	sticks unsalted butter	$2.99
1	12-count package hamburger buns	$1.59
1	12-count package hot dog buns	$1.59
1	head green leaf lettuce	$1.49
2	yellow onions	$0.34
2	heads fresh garlic	$0.78
12	tomatoes	$6.19
10	ears corn	$4.00
1	red onion	$0.79
2	limes	$0.78
1	8-oz. can grated Parmesan	$2.49
1	18-oz. bottle BBQ sauce	$1.39
1	1-lb. box sugar	$1.19
2	heads red cabbage	$2.78
1	box Darjeeling tea bags	$3.50
1	bunch fresh mint	$1.99
1	12-oz. can frozen lemonade	$1.39
2	18-oz. canisters oatmeal	$2.78
1	6-oz. bag dried cranberries	$2.50
1	8-oz. bag chopped walnuts	$2.79
3	7-oz. bars milk chocolate	$5.37
1	16-oz. box graham crackers	$2.00
1	10-oz. bag marshmallows	$1.00
1	10-oz. can coffee	$2.89
TOTAL	(tax not included)	**$82.97**

ALREADY IN YOUR PANTRY: Dijon mustard, Worcestershire, cider vinegar, salt, pepper, paprika, coarse salt, olive oil, cayenne, and oregano

GUESTS BRING: To stay on budget, Benavidez and Locker asked their guests to supply the beer and bourbon.

---

1 12-oz. can frozen lemonade
  Bourbon (optional)

Boil 12 cups water; remove from heat. Add tea, sugar, and mint. Mix well, then cover and let steep for 1 hour. Remove tea; stir in lemonade and serve over ice. Garnish with extra mint. If desired, pour a shot of bourbon in each glass.

cranberry-nut oatmeal
(serves 12)

  6 cups uncooked oatmeal
    (instant or old-fashioned)
1½ cups dried cranberries

1½ cups chopped walnuts
    Butter (optional)

In a 4-qt. pot, bring 10½ cups water to a boil. Stir in oats; return to a boil. Reduce heat to medium; cook about 1 minute for instant oatmeal (5 minutes for old-fashioned oatmeal) or until most of liquid is absorbed. Stir occasionally. Let stand until oatmeal reaches desired consistency; top with cranberries and walnuts. If using, add butter to taste.

Septe

mber

Can't commit to an overblown,
overpriced wedding reception?
Say "I do" to these clever, cost-conscious
ideas that more than make the grade.

JUST MARRIED

THE MENU

tossed salad with
reen's raspberry
vinaigrette

pepperoni and
cheese pizzas

tater tots

scotch-er-roos

chocolate
cupcakes

cotton candy

"get loose" juice

beer

assorted sodas

juice boxes

Guests knew that this celebration
was going to be different when
they opened the report card invite,
which asked them to RSVP by
grading themselves on attendance, social skills, and dancing.

A Touch of Class

When Jessica Murnane and Dan Jividen decided to tie the knot, they broke all the rules. Rather than plan a by-the-book wedding, the couple snuck off to Jamaica, where the marryin' is easy. "We made three decisions on our wedding day," Murnane says. "We picked a cake, a song, and some flowers." The hotel supplied the rest, including witnesses and an officiant. It's not that Murnane doesn't love to fret over an event. (Her Chicago stationery store, Fuss, is named for her desire to spoil *other* people as they plan their own occasions.) But she and Jividen just couldn't see themselves futzing with a florist or auditioning wedding bands, not to mention paying for such a twirled-up affair. Nevertheless, by the time they returned from the island, the newlyweds knew they wanted to stage some kind of celebration. They held off for a year, until Murnane

132 ** PARTY CENTRAL

A study in casual chic, the happy couple couldn't have been more relaxed in their easygoing ensembles. Dan Jividen donned a simple pink polo shirt and cream corduroys (shoes optional), while Jessica Murnane took advantage of end-of-summer sales to snag this flirty strapless frock and white cotton sailor pants from Cynthia Rowley. Her pink prom shoes cost $6 at the Designer Shoe Warehouse.

happened to visit her little brother's school in Columbus, Ohio. Something about its cafeteria triggered good memories and convinced Murnane that she could pull off a first-class bash on a below-average budget. In fact, she and Jividen agreed that the grand total—including decorations, dinner, and drinks for around 100 guests—wouldn't exceed $1,000.

It didn't hurt that the school offered up its lunchroom for free. More important, the reception's location demanded that Murnane keep things unpretentious and affordable. Instead of engraved invitations, for example, she mailed "report cards" that asked guests to grade themselves on attendance. For the table settings, she used simple school supplies—construction paper, encyclopedias, pencils—to create a one-of-a-kind look that eludes most brides.

Figuring out the menu was much easier than suffering through tedious tastings with a caterer. Murnane and Jividen simply ordered parbaked pies from a local pizza joint and hit Sam's Club for salad mix, Tater Tots, and cupcakes. The only from-scratch fare: vinaigrette salad dressing, Scotch-Er-Roos, and a gin-and-sparkling-wine punch. (However, for you, we've provided recipes for almost everything, each scaled back to serve 15 guests.)

Of course, no school dance would be complete without, well, dancing. And in this case, guests got down to CD mixes custom-made for the bride and groom by a pal. When the tempo slowed, most folks cleared the floor—except for Murnane and Jividen. They were busy K-I-S-S-I-N-G, which prompted revelers to raise their glasses in honor of the happy couple, who promised to stick together—for richer or (in this case, not much) poorer.

Tray Chic

Choose the right theme and you can get away with less pretentious (and less expensive) fare. After all, who's gonna expect steak Diane in a school cafeteria? By sticking with classic lunchroom chow—pizza, Tater Tots, a simple tossed salad—Murnane and Jividen managed to feed approximately 100 guests for less than $600 total, which could explain the bride's wide grin, above.

Instead of some multitiered confection topped with a plastic bride and groom, these frosted chocolate charmers, opposite, took the cake. Reminiscent of that lunch box staple, the Hostess Cup Cake, the treats were bought in bulk at Sam's Club and came decorated with mini chalkboards.

A Good Sign

In place of a white engraved leather-bound guest book, Murnane and Jividen laid a three-ring binder and a small children's chalkboard atop a cafeteria table covered in crisp white paper. Balloons, not fancy flower garlands, served as the only decoration.

The bride's sister and her beau, above, jived junior high style—holding on tight but keeping each other at arms length. Left: A young guest swigged her cocktail of choice.

Centerpiece de Résistance

A wedding feast with no towering calla lilies on the dining tables? Murnane said no to fussy, pricey florals and instead transformed humble school supplies into witty, wilt-proof—and extremely wallet-friendly—decorations, opposite.

BOOK SMART: Encyclopedias picked up at a local thrift store for pennies per volume make savvy centerpieces. For each arrangement, Murnane covered one book and glued on a construction paper number to create table markers.

CHEAT SHEET: Peeking was permitted on the pop-quiz place mats the couple designed on their computer. Murnane gave the edges a flourish with a rotary scalloping machine, but it's a breeze to do with pinking shears. An instant icebreaker, the multiple-choice questions (Q: "What was Jessica's campaign slogan for her sixth-grade class election?" A: "J.A.M.! with Jessica Alice Murnane.") got perfect strangers gabbing right away.

TAKE A LESSON: Pages cut from an old science text and mounted on card stock served as holders for pencils personalized with DAN AND JESSICA (around $20 for 100 pencils at MilesKimball .com). On the underside of each card, guests were designated "best dancer," "biggest flirt," etc. by the bride and groom.

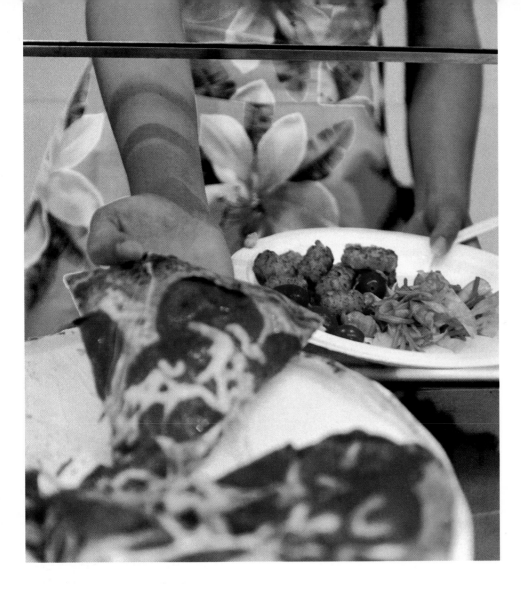

In addition to the pizza and salad, guests helped themselves to Tater Tots. To feed 15 folks, you'll need two 32-ounce bags of Tater Tots. Opposite: A view of the bride through construction-paper-chain curtains she made herself.

Turn onto a lightly floured surface and continue kneading until dough is smooth and elastic, about 10 minutes. (If dough is too sticky, gradually add more flour, 2 to 3 tbsp. at a time.)

Roll dough into a large ball, then cut it into four pieces. Roll each piece into a smooth ball, place on a lightly floured surface in a warm, draft-free area, and cover with a kitchen towel. Let dough rise until doubled in size, about 45 minutes. Meanwhile, place a pizza stone in the center of the oven and preheat to 500°F. (The stone should sit in the oven for at least 30 minutes.) If you don't have a pizza stone, use a cookie sheet.

Holding the dough in your hands, gently stretch it, turning it as you do so to create a 10-inch round. Carefully place on pizza stone or cookie sheet, and brush surface with olive oil. If you plan on serving the pizzas immediately, add a layer of sauce, then a layer of cheese to all four, and pepperoni to two. Bake for 8 to 11 minutes (if you're using a cookie sheet, you may need to let the pizzas bake a

THE RECIPES

tossed salad with reen's raspberry vinaigrette
(serves 15)

- 2 **heads romaine lettuce, ribs removed**
- 1 **head iceberg lettuce**
- 1 **head Boston lettuce, ribs removed**
- 6 **cups shredded, peeled carrots**
- 6 **cups grape tomatoes**
  Reen's Raspberry Vinaigrette (see below)

Tear lettuce into bite-size pieces. Toss with carrots and tomatoes in a large salad bowl. Dress with vinaigrette just before serving.

reen's raspberry vinaigrette
(makes 3¾ cups)

- 8 **cloves garlic, peeled and crushed**
- ¾ **cup honey**
- 1 **tsp. salt, plus more to taste**
- 1 **cup raspberry red wine vinegar**
- 2 **cups extra virgin olive oil**

In a small bowl, combine garlic, honey, and salt. Whisk in vinegar. Add oil in a steady stream, whisking constantly. Let sit for a few hours to allow the flavors to develop. Pour over salad and toss until greens are entirely coated.

pepperoni and cheese pizzas
(makes four 10-inch thin crust pizzas)

- 3 **cups all-purpose flour, plus an additional ¼ to ½ cup for kneading**
- ¾ **cup semolina flour (or another ¾ cup all-purpose flour)**
- 1 **tsp. salt**
- 1 **package (2¼ tsp.) active dry yeast**
- 1½ **tbsp. olive oil, plus more for baking pizza crust**
- 1¼ **cup very warm water (110°F)**
- 3½ **cups tomato sauce (see recipe on page 140)**
- 4 **cups shredded mozzarella cheese**
- 6 **oz. pepperoni, sliced**

In a large mixing bowl, stir together 3 cups all-purpose flour, semolina flour (or ¾ cup all-purpose flour), salt, and yeast. Make a well in the center, pour in olive oil and water, and using a large metal spoon, gradually stir dry ingredients into the liquid. As dough comes together, knead with your hands until all of the flour mixture is incorporated.

little longer), or until cheese is golden. (If you want to serve the pizzas at a later time, parbake the oiled crust for 3 to 4 minutes, or until dough is just set. Cool crusts on a wire baking rack, then place them in a large freezer bag and freeze until you're ready to use them. To bake, place the frozen crusts on a preheated pizza stone or cookie sheet, cover with a layer of sauce and add cheese to all four, pepperoni to two. Leave them in the oven for 8 to 11 minutes, or until cheese is golden.) Cool on a wire rack, then transfer to a cutting board to serve.

tomato sauce
(makes 3½ cups, enough for four 10-inch pizzas)
- 1 28-oz. can crushed tomatoes
- 1 6-oz. can tomato paste
- 1 tsp. garlic powder
- 1 tsp. dried oregano
- ½ tsp. dried basil
- ½ tsp. dried rosemary
- ½ tsp. salt
- ½ tsp. freshly ground black pepper
- ¼ tsp. crushed red pepper

In a large saucepan over medium heat, combine tomatoes and paste with 1 cup water, then add seasonings. Bring to a simmer, stirring. Reduce heat to low and simmer uncovered for 45 minutes, or until the sauce is reduced by a third. The sauce can be made ahead and refrigerated in an airtight container for up to 4 days.

scotch-er-roos
(makes 16)
- 1 cup sugar
- 1 cup light corn syrup
- 1 cup smooth peanut butter
  Butter, for greasing pan
- 6 cups crisped rice cereal
- 1 6-oz. package butter-scotch chips
- 1 8-oz. package semi-sweet chocolate chips

Combine sugar and corn syrup in a large saucepan. Heat over medium heat, stirring, until sugar dissolves. Add peanut butter and stir until smooth. Remove the pan from the stove and pour crisped rice cereal into it. Mix together, stirring gently and quickly. Press it into a

greased 13-by-9-inch brownie pan. Place butter-scotch and chocolate chips in the top of a double boiler set over medium-high heat and melt them together, stirring to prevent burning. Pour melted chips over cereal mixture, covering entire surface. Let cool. Cut into approximately 3 by 2 inch pieces.

chocolate cupcakes
(makes 15 to 20)
- ½ cup unsweetened cocoa powder
- 7 tbsp. boiling water
- ⅔ cup full-fat sour cream, at room temperature
- 2 large eggs, at room temperature
- 1 tsp. almond extract
- 2 cups cake flour
- 1 cup sugar
- ½ cup firmly packed light brown sugar
- ¾ tsp. baking soda
- ½ tsp. salt
- 2 sticks (16 tbsp.) unsalted butter, softened
  Decorator Icing (see recipe at right)

Preheat oven to 350°F and line two muffin tins with paper muffin cups. Whisk

together cocoa powder and boiling water in a small bowl until smooth. Let cool. In another bowl, lightly beat sour cream, eggs, and almond extract together with a fork. In a large mixing bowl, combine flour, sugars, baking soda, and salt. Add butter, and using an electric mixer, beat until butter pieces resemble tiny pebbles. Add half the sour cream mixture and beat on low speed until dry mixture has been incorporated. Mix in remaining sour cream mixture and beat on medium-high speed for 1½ minutes, until thoroughly blended. Add cocoa mixture and continue to beat until batter is smooth and uniform. Fill muffin cups to the top and bake for about 20 minutes, or until a toothpick inserted in the middle of one comes out clean. Let cool, then frost with icing.

decorator icing
(makes enough for 20 cupcakes)
- 2 sticks (16 tbsp.) unsalted butter, softened

Someone spiked the punch…with sparkling wine and gin, opposite, far left. Opposite middle: Murnane and Jividen passed around lunch trays stacked with chewy Scotch-Er-Roos—a far more tempting treat than typical jaw-breaking Jordan almonds. Opposite, right: One guest's present stacked up nicely; an assortment of baking supplies were tucked inside tiers of different-size gift boxes.

Cotton to This Sweet Idea

Rather than force guests to stand idly by and watch the usual matrimonial cake cutting, Murnane and Jividen got 'em in on the act—spinning their own dessert over a cotton candy machine. The couple rented the contraption from a local party-supply store for $60 a day, which included 100 paper cones and seven pounds of Flossugar. Depending on where you live, a similar deal will set you back $60 to $130. Look up PARTY RENTALS or CATERING SUPPLIES in your yellow pages and shop around for the best deal. Be sure to ask if delivery, cones, and sugar are included in the price quote. And if classic strawberry and blueberry don't suit your palate, hit PopcornSupply.com for more exotic flavors like piña colada, blue raspberry, grape, lime, or orange (each $6 carton makes 50 cones).

¼ tsp. salt
2 tsp. vanilla extract
1 16-oz. box confectioners' sugar
1 tbsp. meringue powder
1 tbsp. whole milk
   Red food coloring, as needed

Combine butter, salt, and vanilla in large bowl, and beat with an electric mixer until fluffy. Slowly add sugar, ⅓ cup at a time, beating until combined. Gradually add meringue powder, then milk and turn mixer to high, beating until all ingredients are blended. Add food coloring to achieve the desired hue and continue beating until frosting is light and fluffy, about 6 minutes.

To pipe icing onto cupcakes: Put icing in a pastry bag fitted with a star tip, squeezing all the air out before closing the open end. Pipe icing steadily through the tip, working in a circular pattern from each cupcake's rim to its center.

"get loose" juice
(make 9 cups)

6 lemons, juiced, plus 1 lemon for garnish
1 cup confectioners' sugar
½ 750-ml bottle chilled gin
2 750-ml bottles chilled sparkling wine

Combine lemon juice and sugar in a large punch bowl, mixing until sugar dissolves completely. Add gin and ice. Add sparkling wine slowly to prevent it from fizzing. Stir once or twice. Cut remaining lemon into ¼-inch slices and float on top of the punch.

THE RECEIPT

2 heads romaine lettuce	$2.58
1 head iceberg lettuce	$1.29
1 head Boston lettuce	$0.99
6 large carrots	$0.59
3 pt. grape tomatoes	$5.79
1 12-oz. honey bear	$3.35
1 8-oz. bottle raspberry red wine vinegar	$3.99
1 17-oz. bottle olive oil	$4.99
1 2-lb. bag all-purpose flour	$1.29
1 0.75-oz. package yeast	$1.89
1 16-oz. bag shredded mozzarella	$4.99
6 oz. sliced pepperoni	$3.38
1 28-oz. can crushed tomatoes	$1.49
1 6-oz. can tomato paste	$0.59
2 32-oz. bags Tater Tots	$5.98
1 18-oz. jar peanut butter	$1.59
1 13.5-oz. box crisped rice cereal	$3.69
1 1-lb. box unsalted butter	$4.19
1 11-oz. bag butterscotch chips	$2.79
1 12-oz. bag semisweet chocolate chips	$2.79
1 8-oz. can unsweetened cocoa	$2.39
1 8-oz. tub sour cream	$0.69
1 2-lb. box cake flour	$1.99
1 16-oz. box light brown sugar	$0.89
1 2-lb. bag confectioners' sugar	$1.59
1 8-oz. can meringue powder	$8.99
1 0.5-oz. bottle red food coloring	$1.75
7 lemons	$1.40
1 750-ml bottle gin	$10.00
2 750-ml bottles sparkling wine	$9.98
1 18-pack Miller Light	$13.99
1 2-l bottle diet cola	$0.99
1 2-l bottle cola	$0.99
12 juice boxes	$2.18
TOTAL	**$116.05**
(tax not included)	

ALREADY IN YOUR PANTRY: garlic, salt, semolina flour, garlic powder, oregano, basil, rosemary, pepper, crushed red pepper, sugar, light corn syrup, eggs, almond extract, baking soda, vanilla, milk

To scare up an otherworldly Halloween fright-fest, all you need is a wild imagination— and a wicked sense of humor.

THE MENU
pale-as-a-ghost
cheese plate

deviled egg
eyeballs

turkey finger
sandwiches

ham and spinach
mummy skin
pinwheels

roasted corn and
crawfish mummy
skin pinwheels

skewered beast
with peanut
dipping sauce

innards pasta
alfredo

almond brain
blancmange

piña colada
witches' brew

spellbinding beer

Having a Scream

As the sun went down at 3302 Centenary Boulevard in Shreveport, Louisiana, a thick fog settled in among the headstones. Rows of ghoulish jack-o'-lanterns began to glow, while a half dozen dirt-encrusted skeletons were poised to scale the house's facade. Looming overhead, a gigantic spider watched for unsuspecting prey. All of a sudden, an eyeball the size of a hay bale rolled through the yard with a little girl— wait, no, a teenage boy *dressed* as a little girl—bounding behind it in a short blue tulle skirt. A gaggle of his cross-dressing friends followed, as Donna Summer's "MacArthur Park" blasted through the speakers. Presiding over this outlandish mayhem? Shandu, the all-seeing swami,

Elizabeth and William Joyce, below, got spurred on by a campy cowboy. Opposite: William's spooky artwork covered walls and lamps throughout his home.

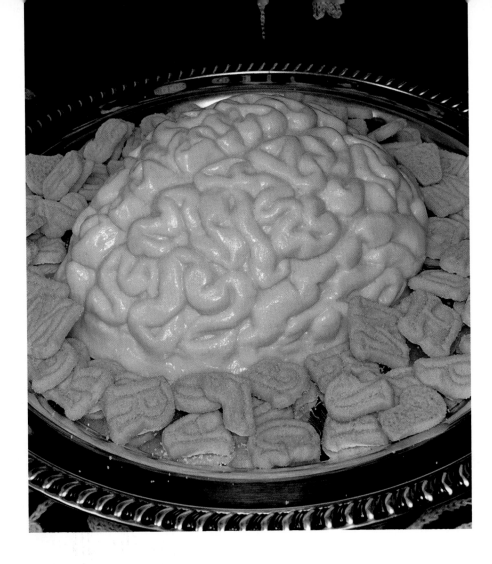

A smart concoction of condensed milk, almond extract, and gelatin, this Almond Brain Blancmange (formed with a mold which cost about $5 at Copabananas.com), left, is so easy to prepare that it's almost an afterthought. Opposite: The Joyce family gave guests a chilly welcome. From left: Ten-year-old Jack played a pint-size Shaquille O'Neal, Elizabeth stared vacantly as a lost soul, and lovely Mary Katherine, 15, crowned herself Miss America.

sporting a single taxidermy eye in his turban.

Welcome to Halloween at the home of illustrator and children's book author William Joyce (a.k.a. Shandu), whose sly dark humor seems to have trumped the holiday's usual blood-and-guts scare tactics. Best known for characters who are as sophisticated as they are silly (Rolie Polie Olie is a robot living on a brightly colored, geometric planet; George Shrinks is a Tom Thumb–size adventurer from the art deco era), Joyce is never simply entertaining the kids.

Nowhere is this more apparent than at the annual Skeletal Ball, hosted by Joyce and his wife, Elizabeth. What started out 15 years ago as a small gathering has since morphed into an all-out community event, drawing some 500 (that's right, 500) guests, ranging in age from 2 to 70—all of them in costume, and *all* of them giddy with a youthful excitement.

And how could they not be? Each year Joyce spends months transforming his property into a fantastically macabre theme park. Nearly 75 jack-o'-lanterns are scattered about the grounds. A pond filled with dry ice (and refilled at least once during the evening) billows smoke as a single skeleton rises from its depths, while fortune-tellers hunch under white canopies,

sharing their visions of the future. Inside the house, shiver-inducing, albeit primarily plastic, spiders crawl over nearly every surface. There's a zombie stalking the buffet table. On the walls, shadowboxes containing voodoolike groupings of bones and shells hang next to cartoonish murals of black silhouettes. And more skeletons lounge lazily on chairs and sofas. ("Buy them in bulk and you get a big discount," advises Joyce, who recently dropped $1,500 on 15 plastic medical-school-grade teaching models.) Clearly, this is a man obsessed.

You might expect someone with two Emmys to his credit (for *Rolie Polie Olie*, which airs on the Disney Channel) to simply call in the Hollywood props department and ask that it stage such a spectacular setup. In actuality, however, many of the artist's tricks are homemade, as well as downright cheap. Okay, Joyce's talent helps (a lot), but regardless of your artistic abilities, the basic how-to is pretty easy: Headstones are sawed from thick Styrofoam called blue board, and the shadowbox collages are basic glue-gun creations framed with scrap wood. As for those eyeballs: They're just exercise balls, spray-painted white and dotted with black pupils.

Gourds of the Manor

Because of their tough skins, dried gourds (dirt cheap at supermarkets and farm stands in the fall) are more difficult to carve than fresh pumpkins. In fact, you'll need to buy a power tool to do it (Joyce uses a RotoZip, about $100 at hardware stores). But the hard work really pays off. Gourds come in lots of shapes and sizes, so they give your doorstep a bigger dose of drama. And instead of rotting right after Halloween, they'll last for many years (and moons).

School-age sorceresses greeted the pond's resident skeleton, above, which "floated" in dry ice. Below: After a night of square dancin', a couple of Texas two-steppers took a breather; you can buy a real framed tarantula like the one next to them for about $30 and up at New York City's Evolution (800-952-3195), or steal it—the idea, that is—with a frame, a glue gun, and a plastic spider.

While Joyce handles all the decor himself, he does call in a Shreveport caterer for help with the provisions (and wisely so, considering the countless characters he has to feed). Even still, he ensures that the menu—a ghostly all-white buffet of appetizer-size nibbles—sticks to the Halloween theme. It includes creepy delights like Mummy Skin Pinwheels stuffed with crawfish and corn or ham and spinach; Turkey Finger Sandwiches; Skewered Beast With Peanut Dipping Sauce (it tastes like chicken); and Innards Pasta Alfredo, a mix of tortellini, tomatoes, and capers. The food is foolproof and kid-friendly, and can all be made ahead of time. Pare the guest list down by, oh, about 475 people, and for a little over $300 (including beer and Piña Colada Witches' Brew), the whole spread is also pretty affordable. Nothing requires much ado or attention—crucial on a night when the goal is to have a good time.

Of course, there's no disputing that everyone always has a *great* time. As Joyce says, "Even the most uptight person will loosen up dressed as something else." And by 10 P.M., when, as he puts it, "people have drunk just enough to really forget who they are," the adults start to enjoy themselves even more than the kids. But why, when it's over in mere hours, would anyone go to so much trouble?

"Halloween is the only night all year when life feels more like a movie," Joyce explains. "It is art directed, and I score it. There are special effects and a cast of hundreds—and you never know how it's going to end."

You Dig?

No family plots on your estate? Not to worry. A haunting Halloween cemetery is only a weekend project away. To make each headstone, you'll need to start with a four-by-eight-foot sheet of four-inch-thick Styrofoam called blue board (look in the yellow pages under PLASTICS SUPPLIERS to find a good source). First, trace on a hair-raising shape and carve it out with a fine-tooth jigsaw. Then to give the headstone a weathered look, use a cheap paintbrush and dab on a bit of acetone here and there. (Sold at most hardware stores, acetone is very noxious and should only be handled by adults. Apply it to the tombstone in a well-ventilated area and be sure to wear a mask and gloves.) Next, paint the surface with several coats of light gray water-based acrylic, working the paint into the pores of the foam. Once that's dry, add details with permanent markers and spray paint. (Joyce recommends Design Master brand floral sprays, available at AFloral .com, because they won't eat into the foam.) Finally, sink two metal rods (an eighth of an inch in diameter and three to four feet long; available at most hardware stores) three-quarters of the way into the bottom of the headstone. Turn the stone upright and sink the exposed rods into the ground, propping up the gravestone with rocks and bricks. The finishing touch: a fresh mound of dirt.

Cheaper Creepers!

Although the monstrous spider, above, was neither simple nor inexpensive, Joyce's party does offer up plenty of clever, low-cost ideas that nearly anyone can copy:

KEEP YOUR EYE ON THE BALL Joyce's Rolie Polie eyeballs, above, are big rubber exercise and playground balls in disguise (Constructive Playthings sells balls in different sizes for about $10 to $25 each; www.constplay.com). The artist sprayed on several coats of a water-based primer in flat white, then, when dry, brushed in the pupil with a water-based acrylic in flat black.

DIVINE INTERVENTION The fortune-tellers Joyce hired for his party, left, were wildly popular and, at $100 an hour, pretty pricey. But even your friend and her Magic 8 Ball can work wonders if given a proper lair. Try using an ethereal mosquito-net bed canopy like the one Bed Bath & Beyond sells for about $30. As for a soothsaying surface, any old table will do, though Joyce conjured up an enchanted forest feel with a faux stump.

OCCULT CLASSICS To make a shadowbox like the one above, all you'll need are some plywood scraps, toy skeletons, and a glue gun. Cut a piece of plywood for the background and nail on a frame of four-inch-wide-by-one-inch-thick boards. (Joyce likes to first stain the background piece with a raw umber water-based acrylic paint.) Then secure the skeletons and other cursed curios (sold at discount stores come holiday time or at Einsteins-Emporium.com for $2 to $8 apiece) with a glue gun. Finally, prop up your box or hang it by attaching picture wire to the back.

PRIDE OF FRANKENSTEIN Why give up the cold-spaghetti-intestines-in-a-bowl kind of fun just because you're an adult? Though any clear vessel will take on a grim glow with the addition of water and red food coloring, you can find real lab glass, like the pieces at right, on eBay for $20 and up. For an added effect, sink plastic skulls into the tinted liquid and let toy spiders climb the walls with the help of blue poster putty.

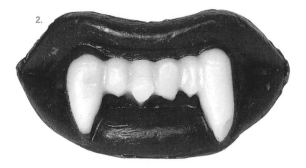

Ghoulish Goodies

As the Joyces' Skeletal Ball attests, Halloween is all about outlandish creativity. So instead of stocking your candy bowl with typical mini Snickers, surprise trick-or-treaters with these quirky confections of yesteryear. All are available for cheap, in bulk, at DiscountCandy.com.

1. LIPSTICKS Pucker up, buttercup. These sour-cherry wands have been tempting lips since the '50s.

2. WAX FANGS Talk about love at first bite! These '20s-era kissers (which double as snappy costume accessories) now come flavored with cinnamon.

3. GOLD MINE At about one buck each, a two-ounce sack of nuggets ain't a steal, but it does offer a faux-gold mother lode of banana-bubble-gum goodness.

4. CIGARETTES Political correctness dictates that these sugar smokes now be called "candy sticks," but the smartly designed boxes remain addictive.

5. BLACK TAFFY Although this '70s taffy is actually tri-colored, its licorice taste is pure black magic.

6. NECCO WAFERS First rolled out in 1901, these iconic crisp discs come in eight funky flavors.

7. ASTRO POP This lolly's three luscious layers—cherry, passion fruit, and pineapple—are delightfully exotic.

8. POP ROCKS Chasing this fizzy carbonated candy with a gulp of Coke still feels sizzlingly illicit. The rocks have been scaring parents since 1975.

Newlyweds toast the Day of the Dead, above left. Above right: turkey sandwiches, assorted pinwheels, and chicken kebabs.

THE RECIPES

Clay and Nita Cook, the husband-and-wife team behind Cook's Culinary Company in Shreveport, Louisiana, devised the Skeletal Ball's menu. The recipes below will feed at least 25 guests.

deviled egg eyeballs
(makes 72)

- **3 dozen eggs**
- **1 cup mayonnaise**
- **3 tbsp. yellow mustard**
- **3 tbsp. sweet pickle relish**
- **3 tbsp. dill relish**
- **Salt and pepper, to taste**
- **1 15-oz. can sliced black olives**

Divide eggs between two Dutch ovens, cover with cold water, and bring water to a gentle simmer over medium heat; continue to simmer for 15 minutes. Check an egg for doneness, then drain water and allow eggs to cool. Peel off shells, slice eggs lengthwise, and remove yolks. Arrange whites on a serving tray. In a large mixing bowl, combine yolks with mayo, mustard, relishes, salt, and pepper, and mix until smooth. Using a spoon (or a pastry bag with a large, plain tip), fill egg whites with yolk mixture. Garnish each egg with a slice of black olive.

turkey finger sandwiches (makes 96)

- **Mayonnaise, to taste**
- **48 slices white bread**
- **3 lb. smoked turkey, sliced thin**

Spread mayonnaise on each slice of bread. Layer half the slices with 2 oz. turkey each, then top with remaining bread. Place sandwiches in stacks of three and trim crusts, then cut stacks into quarters.

ham and spinach mummy skin pinwheels
(makes 96)

- **2 cups pecans**
- **2 lb. cream cheese, softened**
- **¾ cup sour cream**
- **2 tsp. Creole or Cajun seasoning**
- **12 12-inch flour (or sun-dried tomato) tortillas**

- **1½ lb. ham, sliced thin**
- **1 5-oz. bag baby spinach leaves**

In a 350°F oven, toast pecans on a baking sheet until they're lightly browned, about 5 minutes. In a medium bowl, mix together cream cheese, sour cream, and Creole or Cajun seasoning. Set aside. Layer tortillas between damp paper towels and microwave on high for about 20 seconds, or until soft. Spread a thin layer of cream cheese mixture on each tortilla, all the way to the edges. With tortilla lying flat, place a row of toasted pecans down the left side of the tortilla (stopping about an inch from the top and bottom), a row of ham down the center, and a layer of baby spinach leaves on top of the ham. Fold in about 1 inch of the top and bottom of each tortilla, then, beginning with pecan side, roll filled tortilla up tightly. Refrigerate 2 to 3 hours or overnight. Using a sharp knife, cut each rolled tortilla into 8 slices.

roasted corn and crawfish mummy skin pinwheels
(makes 96)

- **4 cups frozen corn, defrosted and drained**
- **8 tbsp. olive oil**
- **2 lb. cream cheese, softened**
- **¾ cup sour cream**
- **4 tsp. Creole or Cajun seasoning**
- **2 lb. frozen crawfish tail meat, defrosted (or use 2 lb. cooked shrimp, peeled and deveined)**
- **12 12-inch flour (or spinach) tortillas**
- **1 5-oz. bag baby spinach leaves**

Preheat oven to 400°F. Spread corn kernels on a baking sheet and drizzle with olive oil; roast, stirring often, for about 20 minutes, or until lightly browned. In a medium bowl, mix together cream cheese, sour cream, and 2 tsp. Creole or Cajun seasoning. In another bowl, mix remaining seasoning with

crawfish. Set both aside. Layer tortillas between damp paper towels and microwave on high for about 20 seconds, or until soft. Spread a thin layer of cream cheese mixture on each tortilla, all the way to the edges. With tortilla lying flat, sprinkle entire surface with roasted corn, then place a row of crawfish down the left side of the tortilla (stopping about an inch from the top and bottom) and a row of baby spinach leaves down the center. Fold in about 1 inch of the top and bottom of each tortilla, then, beginning with crawfish side, roll filled tortilla up tightly. Refrigerate 2 to 3 hours or overnight. Using a sharp knife, cut each rolled tortilla into 8 slices.

skewered beast with peanut dipping sauce

(makes about 30 skewers)

- 15 boneless, skinless chicken breasts
  Olive oil, as needed
  Creole or Cajun seasoning, to taste
- 30 6-inch bamboo skewers
  Peanut Dipping Sauce (see recipe at right)

Preheat oven to 350ºF. Meanwhile, drizzle chicken breasts with olive oil and sprinkle with seasoning. Heat a 12-inch skillet over high heat, and working in batches, add chicken and brown for 2 to 3 minutes per side. (Add about 2 tbsp. olive oil to the skillet between batches.) Transfer chicken to a baking dish and bake for 15 minutes,

or until cooked through. Allow chicken to cool, then cut each in half lengthwise and each half into bite-size chunks. Spear a few chunks on a skewer and serve with dipping sauce.

peanut dipping sauce (makes 6 cups)

- 4 cups crunchy peanut butter
- 1 cup hot chicken broth
- 1 cup cream of coconut
  Cayenne pepper, to taste

Place all ingredients in a food processor (or blender, working in batches) and pulse to mix.

innards pasta alfredo

(makes 25 appetizer-size portions)

- 8 cups heavy cream
- 4 tsp. (about 4 cloves) minced fresh garlic
- 4 cups shredded Parmesan cheese
- 4 medium tomatoes, seeded, diced, and drained
- 1 cup capers, drained
- 4 lb. fresh cheese tortellini, cooked until tender and drained

In a Dutch oven, bring cream and garlic to a boil. Reduce heat to medium-low and simmer until cream cooks down by about a third, stirring often to prevent it from burning, about 15 minutes. Gradually add cheese, whisking until smooth. Fold in remaining ingredients and serve hot in a chafing dish (or refrigerate and reheat to serve later).

An all-white selection of Brie wedges and cubed cheddar and Swiss, left, was served with crackers and grapes; for $100 or more at FrightCatalog.com, you can splurge on a zombie to protect the spread. Opposite: Deviled Egg Eyeballs sated two- *and* eight-legged guests.

THE RECEIPT

2 lb. Brie cheese	$11.98
2 lb. cheddar cheese	$11.98
2 lb. Swiss cheese	$11.98
3 5-oz. boxes water crackers	$5.37
2 lb. green grapes	$3.98
3 dozen eggs	$3.99
1 18-oz. jar mayonnaise	$2.79
1 15-oz. can sliced black olives	$2.39
3 loaves white bread	$4.47
3 lb. sliced smoked turkey	$17.97
1 1/2-lb. bag pecans	$3.50
8 8-oz. bars cream cheese	$9.52
1 16-oz. tub sour cream	$1.29
1 8-oz. jar Creole seasoning	$1.75
3 10-count packages 12-inch flour tortillas	$3.87
1.5 lb. sliced ham	$8.99
2 5-oz. bags baby spinach leaves	$6.58
1 32-oz. bag frozen corn	$2.45
2 1-lb. bags frozen crawfish tail meat	$17.98
15 boneless, skinless chicken breasts	$31.50
1 100-count package 6-inch bamboo skewers	$0.49
3 28-oz. jars crunchy peanut butter	$11.79
1 14.25-oz. can chicken broth	$0.99
2 15-oz. cans cream of coconut	$5.00
2 1-qt. cartons heavy cream	$7.98
3 5-oz. bags shredded Parmesan cheese	$9.75
4 medium tomatoes	$1.90
1 8-oz. jar capers	$2.99
4 lb. fresh cheese tortellini	$23.96
1 1-oz. box unflavored gelatin	$1.39
2 14-oz. cans sweetened condensed milk	$4.18
1 24-oz. box animal crackers	$3.99
1 1/2-gallon carton orange juice	$1.59
1 1/2-gallon carton pineapple juice	$3.19
1 1.75-l bottle rum	$21.99
1 2-l bottle ginger ale	$0.99
3 24-packs Corona beer	$44.94
TOTAL (tax not included)	**$311.44**

ALREADY IN YOUR PANTRY: yellow mustard, sweet pickle relish, dill relish, salt, pepper, olive oil, cayenne, garlic, vegetable oil, almond extract

almond brain blancmange
(serves 25)

- ¾ oz. (3 packets) gelatin
- 2½ cups cold water
- Vegetable oil, as needed
- 2½ cups sweetened condensed milk
- 2 tsp. almond extract

In a medium-size metal bowl, sprinkle gelatin over cold water and let sit for 1 hour. Meanwhile, lightly grease the inside of a brain-shaped mold (available at Copabananas .com for around $5) with vegetable oil. Place the bowl over a larger saucepan filled with simmering water (or use a double boiler), and stir constantly, heating just until gelatin dissolves (do not allow mixture to boil). Remove from heat, and stir in milk and almond extract. Pour mixture into mold and refrigerate overnight. Unmold onto a platter and serve with animal crackers or alphabet cookies.

piña colada witches' brew
(makes enough to fill 2 large punch bowls: 1 alcoholic; 1 nonalcoholic)

- 6 cups orange juice
- 6 cups pineapple juice
- 1 15-oz. can cream of coconut
- 4 cups light rum
- 1 2-l bottle ginger ale

Divide juices and cream of coconut between two large punch bowls; stir well. Add rum to taste in one of the punch mixtures (for the adults' punch). Divide ginger ale between mixtures and top both with ice.

November

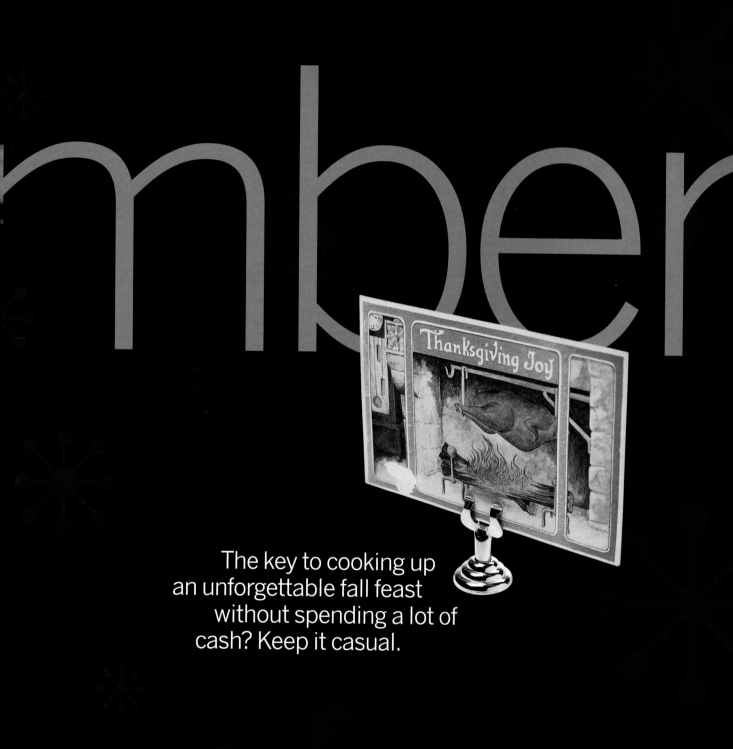

mber

Thanksgiving Joy

The key to cooking up an unforgettable fall feast without spending a lot of cash? Keep it casual.

THE MENU

red radishes with
butter and salt

homemade
potato chips

grilled sweet
italian sausage

fried livers with
quick-pickled
red onion

grilled capons

bibb lettuce
with buttermilk
dressing

sautéed butternut
squash and pears
with thyme and
candied bacon

gabrielle's
stovetop stuffing

cranberry sauce

pumpkin fool

assorted pies

wine

Hamilton, below (in a light blue jacket), and her guests unpacked the car in preparation for 24 deliciously laid-back hours of cooking, eating, and snoozing.

A Movable Feast

On Thanksgiving morning, you won't find chef Gabrielle Hamilton leaning into her oven, basting a turkey. She doesn't set up card tables or polish sterling silver serving platters. Instead, while most folks are stressing over side dishes, she's usually cruising north on New York's Saw Mill River Parkway, part of a rowdy caravan headed upstate for the day. With only 24 hours off—on the ultimate busman's holiday for a busy restaurateur—Hamilton isn't about to slave over a hot stove. Which isn't to say that she and her guests ever go hungry. Hamilton is, after all, the powerhouse behind Prune, the tiny 30-seat Manhattan bistro that has even the snobbiest uptown foodies lining up on an East Village street corner. It's just that a chef blessed with enough down-to-earth daring to put Triscuit appetizers and

Instead of a corny cornucopia, why not decorate the table with vintage honeycomb turkeys (okay, so a peacock snuck into this flock)? All three of these paper gobblers were snared on eBay for less than $20.

Once the groceries were unloaded, guests got the fireplace going, then kicked back on the couch or sat on sleeping bags to sip drinks and snack on radishes.

Ovaltine-flavored ice cream on the menu isn't likely to be intimidated by one silly little food tradition.

"It's a rare day off. It is not the occasion to try out my new flambé," Hamilton says with typical candor. Nor is it the time, in her opinion, for obligations. Rather than using Thanksgiving to fulfill familial duties, she celebrates with friends. Every year, a core group of five, plus new acquaintances and strays lacking plans, spend the day (and night) together at the no-frills Hudson Valley country house of Hamilton's business partner, Eric Anderson. On their agenda: lots of lounging, drinks before noon, great food, rousing parlor games, and, for a few energetic souls, a late-night walk in the woods before climbing into bed. Early the next morning, after a breakfast of leftover dessert, the sated set heads back to the city.

For the feast itself, Hamilton sticks to a menu that's elegant yet easy and cheap, feeding each guest for about 10 bucks. "I am frugal by nature," she admits. Given that the cook finds turkey grossly overrated, the main course is capon (that's neutered rooster), brined, then grilled. It's a bit more expensive, but Hamilton makes good use of the birds, serving the livers as an hors d'oeuvre. The same oil used to fry the livers also crisps potato chips, as well as bread for the stuffing, which is made on the stovetop with apples, sausages, and sage. As for dessert, Pumpkin Fool is a quick, no-bake complement to guest-brought pies. And mismatched plates and mason jars replace china and crystal on the table.

The steadfast tradition of nontradition, however, is always the most vital component of Hamilton's gatherings. "With this group, there are no rules. No one tells you where to sit. And no one is your mother," she explains. "We have time for conversation, rather than idle 'gee, this food is good' chatter. We actually enjoy ourselves all day long." And for a chef with very little downtime, *that's* something to be thankful for.

Chip In

You might not need industrial-size coffee filters for your morning cup, but the ruffled rounds can do more than strain grounds. Hamilton uses them to drain and then serve homemade potato chips.

Rules of Play

Trivial Pursuit is fun—until you memorize all the answers and misplace all the pie pieces. Hamilton's favorite parlor game, loosely based on TV's *The $100,000 Pyramid*, requires only paper, pens, and a hat.

1. Everyone scribbles categories (songs by the Eagles, things that are fuzzy, reasons to break up) on slips of paper and tosses them into a hat.

2. The group divides into teams of two, with couples separated to prevent short-hand ("your sister's goldfish") and divorce. One team is chosen to go first.

3. A member of that team draws a slip of paper, then calls out clues ("Desperado," "Witchy Woman"), while his or her partner tries to guess the category—in less than a minute.

4. If the partner gets it right, the team scores a point (and continues to draw until the minute is up). The game is over when there are no more slips of paper in the hat.

Sew Thankful

Transform plain white cloth napkins (these were less than $3 each at Pier One) with colorful embroidery floss that spells out THANKS in various foreign languages. The needlework will take some time (not to mention a steady hand), but it's guaranteed to keep your guests in stitches for years to come.

Where there's smoke, there's fiery conversation. Rather than locking herself away in the kitchen, Hamilton—wielding the tongs, of course—turned the preparation of the meal into a social activity.

Hamilton lowered the grocery bill (without messing up the menu) by asking guests, like Anita Essenhauer, above, to contribute pies and wine.

Grilled sweet sausages get a kick from tangy and spicy Dijon mustard.

THE RECIPES

red radishes with butter and salt

(serves 10)
- **3 bunches (about 3 dozen) round red radishes**
- **4 tbsp. unsalted butter**
- **Coarse salt, for dipping**

Wash and trim radishes, leaving about an inch of green stem on top, then refrigerate. Spread butter in a small dish and allow it to soften slightly at room temperature. Serve radishes cold with softened butter and salt (in a separate dish).

homemade potato chips (serves 10)
- **Vegetable oil**
- **5 russet potatoes**
- **Coarse salt, to taste**
- **Red wine vinegar, to taste**

Heat 3 to 4 inches of oil in a deep, heavy-bottomed pot (Hamilton uses a wok) over medium heat. Wash but don't peel potatoes, and use a mandoline to cut them

crosswise into transparent slices. (Bed Bath & Beyond sells one for around $50.) When oil begins to shimmer but is not quite smoking (about 350°F on a candy thermometer), add slices in batches, cooking until golden brown and crisp, about 3 minutes. Remove with a slotted spoon and drain on several layers of coffee filters. While chips are still warm, toss with salt, then sprinkle with vinegar. Reserve oil.

grilled sweet italian sausage (serves 10)
- **1 lb. sweet Italian sausage**
- **Dijon mustard, for dipping**
- **1 12-oz. jar cornichons**

Place charcoal in a grill and ignite. Arrange sausages on the rack and cook for 7 to 8 minutes, turning occasionally, until just cooked through. (Keep the coals lit

Sometimes the store-bought version is better than anything you could make yourself. Every year, Hamilton slides Ocean Spray's cranberry sauce straight from the can into a dish.

Cut to the Chase

You could call 'em batonnets or just plain easy. These three basic steps will turn squat butternut squash and Comice pears into the slender spears that costar in Hamilton's update on traditional sweet potatoes, opposite.

1. Begin by slicing off the tip and tail of your squash or pear. Then cut the neck away from the base. With a vegetable peeler, carefully remove the skin from each piece.

2. Cut each piece of squash or pear in half lengthwise (for squash, you'll want to scoop out any seeds). Next, set the pieces on the cutting board with your most recent cut facing down.

3. Carefully slice both the base and neck pieces lengthwise into ½-inch-wide slices. Then set the slices flat and cut again into ½-inch-thick, frylike sticks.

for cooking the capons later). Serve sausages with mustard and cornichons on the side.

fried livers with quick-pickled red onion (serves 10)

        Reserved vegetable oil
    1   small red onion, sliced into thin slivers
        Coarse salt, to taste
        Red wine vinegar
    2   capon livers
    1   lb. chicken livers
    1½ cups all-purpose flour
        Salt and pepper, to taste

After frying the chips and the bread for the stuffing (see pages 167 and 170), reheat oil to 350°F. Meanwhile, place onion slivers in a small bowl, add coarse salt liberally, then pour red wine vinegar to

cover. Set aside. Rinse livers, drain on a paper towel, then dredge in flour. When oil begins to shimmer, add livers in batches, frying until golden brown, 4 to 5 minutes. Drain on coffee filters and season with salt and pepper. Lift onion slivers out of vinegar and serve with hot livers.

bibb lettuce with buttermilk dressing
(serves 10)

    2   shallots, sliced
    1   clove garlic, chopped
    1   cup mint leaves, roughly chopped
    1   tsp. pepper
        Pinch salt
    1   lemon, juiced
    2   heaping cups mayonnaise
    1½ cups buttermilk

    4   heads Bibb lettuce, washed

Place all ingredients except lettuce in a blender and puree. Tear lettuce and put in a large bowl; drizzle with dressing and toss to coat.

sautéed butternut squash and pears with thyme and candied bacon
(serves 10)

    2   large butternut squash (about 4 lb.)
    3   Comice pears, fairly firm
    1   lemon, juiced
    ½   lb. bacon, cut into ¾-inch cubes
    1   cup light brown sugar
        Cooking spray
    6   tbsp. unsalted butter
    8   sprigs thyme, stems removed

        Salt and pepper, to taste

Preheat oven to 375°F. Cut squash and pears into batonnets (see directions above). If not cooking squash right away, cover with damp paper towels and refrigerate until ready to use. Place pears in a bowl with lemon juice, add water to cover, and set aside. Meanwhile, toss bacon with brown sugar to coat. Place a piece of foil (shiny side up) on a cookie sheet and coat evenly with cooking spray. Coat a second piece and set aside. Spread bacon over cookie sheet in a single layer and bake for 10 to 15 minutes, until sugar has caramelized. With a pair of tongs, immedi-

Sautéed pears and butternut squash may seem like strange bowlfellows, but the combination puts sweet potatoes and marshmallows to shame.

Who says Thanksgiving has to be a stuffy family holiday? Not Hamilton, who encouraged guests to lounge in their pj's all day and drink from mason jars.

THE RECEIPT

3 bunches radishes	$2.37
1/2 lb. unsalted butter	$2.69
5 russet potatoes	$3.12
2 lb. sweet Italian sausage	$9.98
1 12-oz. jar cornichons	$2.59
1 red onion	$0.69
2 8-lb. capons	$32.00
1 lb. chicken livers	$0.99
2 shallots	$0.60
1 bunch mint	$1.49
2 lemons	$1.38
1 18-oz. jar mayonnaise	$2.89
1 pt. buttermilk	$1.19
4 heads Bibb lettuce	$5.96
2 butternut squash	$3.69
3 Comice pears	$2.24
1/2 lb. bacon	$2.00
1 1-lb. box light brown sugar	$0.89
1 bunch thyme	$1.79
1 1-lb. loaf country white bread	$2.79
2 yellow onions	$1.03
1 bunch celery	$1.29
2 Granny Smith apples	$1.49
1 bunch sage	$1.79
2 16-oz. cans Ocean Spray cranberry sauce	$2.78
1 16-oz. carton heavy cream	$2.99
1 1.87-lb. can Libby's Easy Pumpkin Pie Mix	$1.59
TOTAL	**$94.30**
(tax not included)	

ALREADY IN YOUR PANTRY: coarse salt, vegetable oil, red wine vinegar, Dijon mustard, flour, salt, pepper, garlic, sugar, cooking spray, kosher salt

GUESTS BRING: pies, wine

ately transfer bacon to prepared foil to cool. In a large skillet, melt butter over medium heat. When it begins to foam, add squash and stir to coat, cooking until it begins to soften, 3 to 4 minutes. Add pears, along with 4 tbsp. lemon water. Turn heat up to medium-high, cover, and allow mixture to steam until just cooked through, 2 to 3 minutes. Uncover, turn heat up to high, and cook off some of the liquid to make a butter glaze. Remove pan from heat, sprinkle on bacon and thyme, and season with salt and pepper.

gabrielle's stovetop stuffing (serves 10)

- 1 1-lb. loaf good country white bread, torn into bite-size pieces
  Reserved vegetable oil
- 3 tbsp. unsalted butter
- 1 lb. sweet Italian sausage, removed from casings
- 2 yellow onions, chopped
- 2 stalks celery, sliced crosswise into ¼-inch-thick pieces
- 2 Granny Smith apples, quartered and cored (with peels on) and then cut into 1-inch cubes
- 6 sage leaves, cut crosswise into ¼-inch ribbons
  Salt and pepper, to taste

Working in batches, fry bread (in 350°F potato chip oil; see page 167) until golden brown and crisp. Remove with a slotted spoon, drain on coffee filters, and set aside. (Reserve oil to cook livers.) In a large skillet, melt butter over medium-high heat. Brown sausage in butter, stirring occasionally, until completely cooked. Remove sausage with a slotted spoon and set aside. Add onions and celery to remaining fat and sauté, stirring occasionally, until soft. Add apples and ¼ cup water to onion mixture, scraping any bits from the bottom of the pan with a wooden spoon. When apples begin to render liquid, turn heat up high and evaporate all moisture (to prevent bread from becoming soggy). Return sausage to pan; add sage ribbons. Add bread and toss to combine. Season with salt and pepper; serve hot.

pumpkin fool
(serves 10)

- 2 cups heavy cream
- 1 1.87-lb. can Libby's Easy Pumpkin Pie Mix

In a large mixing bowl, whip cream until peaks are stiff. Place pumpkin pie mix in a separate bowl. Gradually fold in whipped cream, reserving 1½ cups for garnish. Place 10 ramekins on a cookie sheet, fill each with mixture, then cover and refrigerate (along with remaining whipped cream) for at least 1 hour. Garnish each with reserved cream and serve.

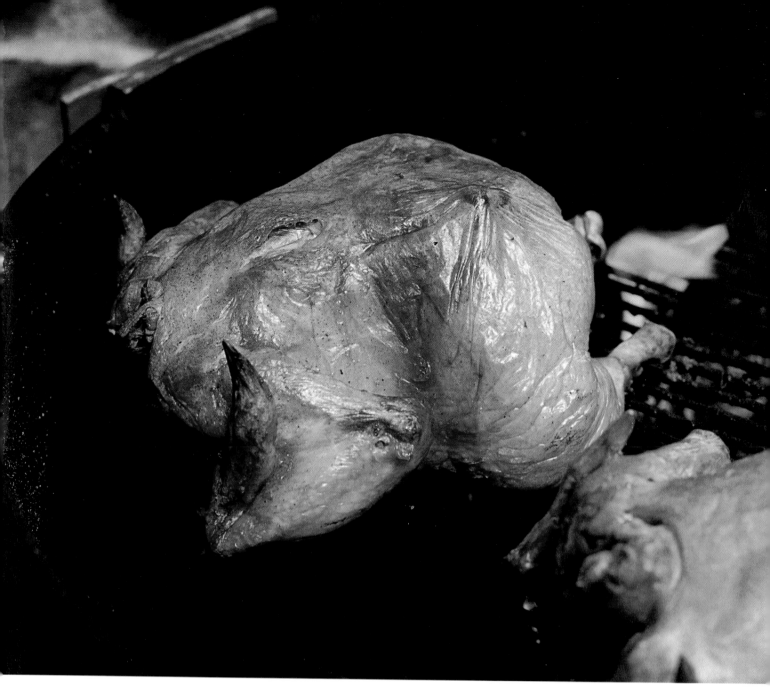

The Capon Countdown

Capons—young roosters that are castrated, then fattened—are known for their tender, flavorful meat. Weighing anywhere from 4 to 13 pounds, they make an excellent replacement for turkey, especially when grilled. To feed 10 people, Hamilton cooked two 8-pound capons.

24 HOURS BEFORE: Place capons in a large pot (Hamilton uses a 5-gallon plastic utility bucket). Add 1 cup sugar, 2 cups kosher salt, and water to cover. Refrigerate (or place outside if it's cold enough).

4 HOURS BEFORE: Get the grill going. When the coals have turned gray, about 45 minutes, use tongs to arrange them in a ring around the grill's outer edge. Place an aluminum pie plate filled with water in the center of the coals to create a space of indirect heat for cooking capons.

3 HOURS BEFORE: Rinse capons and pat dry, then spread a thin layer of vegetable oil over each bird and season with pepper.

Center capons over pie pan on grill, breast side down and horizontally across grill wires (so that the legs don't fall through). Cover grill and cook for 2 to 2½ hours, replenishing coals and water in pan as necessary.

1 HOUR BEFORE: After the birds have been cooking for 2 hours, begin checking them for doneness. Legs should be tender and move easily in their sockets. When the thickest part of the leg joint is pierced, juices should run clear. Allow capons to rest for 20 minutes before carving.

OVEN VARIATION: Place a large foil lasagna pan on the bottom rack of the oven and fill halfway with water. Preheat oven to 350°F. Place brined and seasoned capons directly on the center oven rack, breast side down and horizontally across rack (head and legs will face sides of oven). Roast for 2 hours, checking for doneness after 1½ hours.

1.

2.

3.

The Secret Is out of the Bottle

You probably know that Marc Jacobs designs a lower-priced clothing line called Marc. But unless you're a cork dork, you may not be aware that the wine world has its own version of "second labels." Made from the fruit of average slopes, younger vines, or overabundant harvests, these bottles are given the same TLC as their top-tier brethren—for a fraction of the price. Most of our picks are available at SherryLehmann.com or SamsWine.com.

1. PINOT NOIR The top pinot from California's Kent Rasmussen works wonders with this finicky grape but costs $28 a bottle. Its sibling, Ramsay, just $14, is a by-the-glass favorite at restaurants.

2. CHIANTI Grapes grown near a baron's Tuscan castle go into the top-notch Castello di Brolio Chianti Classico ($40), while a wider selection is used for Barone Ricasoli Rocca Guicciarda Riserva ($18)—a succulent Chianti at half the price.

3. MALBEC Originally a blending grape for Bordeaux, this grape went solo in Nicolas Catena's Catena ($20). His Alamos shows the grape's spiciness and suppleness but sports a $10 price tag.

4. BORDEAUX If you're craving the opulence and cachet of a rich Bordeaux, try Carruades de Lafite ($33), the second label wine from the famed Château Lafite Rothschild.

5. SAUVIGNON BLANC New Zealand's Vavasour does a delicious Single Vineyard Sauvignon Blanc for $27. But at $12, its second label, Dashwood, has the same crispness and a note of green apple.

6. CABERNET SAUVIGNON A Stag's Leap S.L.V. Cabernet ($110) from California is famous for besting its fine French cousins during a blind tasting in 1976. The winery's second label, Hawk Crest, also offers a cabernet with hints of black cherry and spice for an affordable $13.

4.

5.

6.

Dece

mber

Happy Holidays

The classy manse, the fine
furnishings, the family silver—
down South, they're just fancy wrappings
for a Christmas get-together that's
surprisingly unfussy and frugal.

It may look fancy from outside, below, but this chic Southern soiree was really just a simple little shindig at heart. Opposite: Hostess Peggy Pierrepont borrowed a Marx Brothers one-liner for her holiday card.

COME ON IN, Y'ALL

Some say that Southerners have a genetic predisposition for entertaining, but those who hail from below the Mason-Dixon Line know better: It comes from years of hearing their sweet but saucy mothers greet anyone who showed up after 5 P.M. with "Come on in and have a drink!" For this purpose, there was always a tin of spicy cheese straws in the pantry and a fifth of decent bourbon in the decanter. Such gatherings sparkled with capricious energy, primarily because the hostess hadn't gone to too much trouble. After all, who wants to touch canapés from a tray that looks like it took days to arrange? Nothing kills a good time like planned perfection. And it doesn't take one bit of Dixie DNA to understand that.

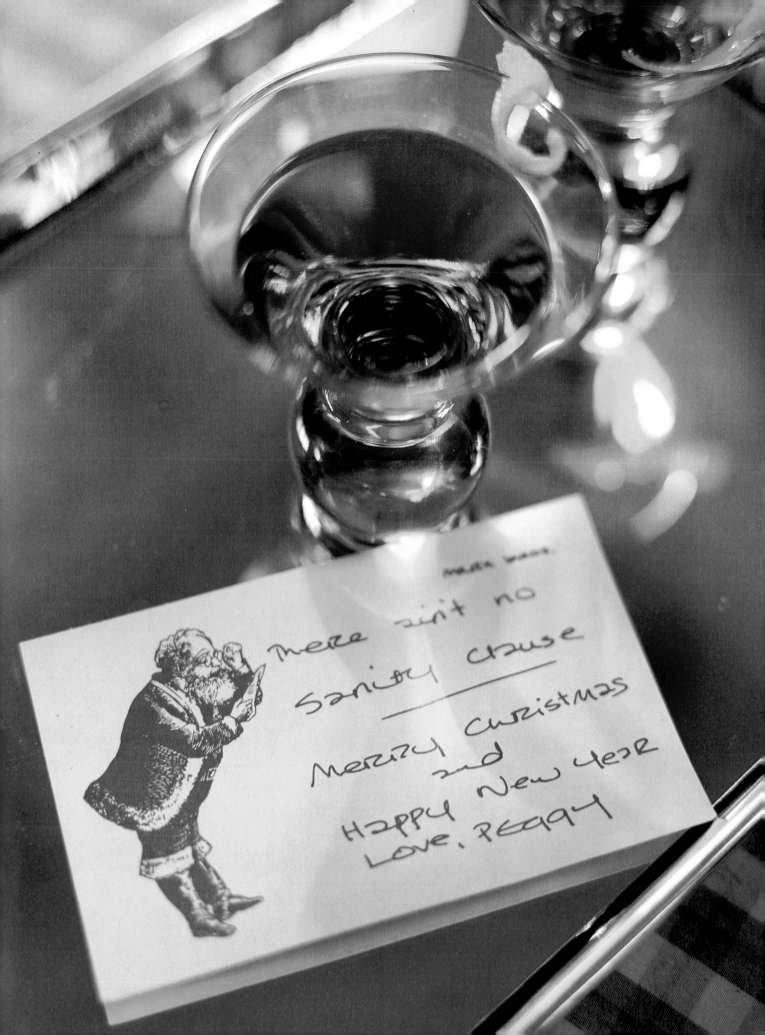

Get Down (South)!

Pierrepont spared her guests the usual holiday hits by the likes of Kenny G and played a mix of seasonal tunes that sound cool no matter what the season.

Christmas in Dixie
ALABAMA

Back Door Santa
CLARENCE CARTER

Blue Christmas
ELVIS PRESLEY

Mixed Nuts
DR. JOHN

Christmas in New Orleans
LOUIS ARMSTRONG

I've Got My Love to Keep Me Warm
BILLIE HOLIDAY

Five Pound Box of Money
PEARL BAILEY

I'll Be Home for Christmas
FATS DOMINO

Baby, It's Cold Outside
ANN-MARGARET AND AL HIRT

What Are You Doing New Year's Eve?
ELLA FITZGERALD

Just ask Peggy Pierrepont, a native New Yorker who moved down to Natchez, Mississippi, in 1995. She was passing through one day, stopped for a quick bite to eat, and never left. "The people here are so warm and friendly," she explains. "And it's the guests who make a party; the hostess just provides a roof."

Pierrepont and local chef Courtney Taylor planned this holiday soiree for 15 friends by following Natchez tradition—both in terms of the budget ($100, including the drinks) and the menu, filled with the same down-to-earth hors d'oeuvres that folks here have served for generations. Not only is the food inexpensive and easy to prepare ahead of time, it also calls for ingredients you can find at any grocery store.

At least three of these party snacks are practically effortless, keep well in a tin, and taste great with bourbon. Salt-Roasted and Spicy Sugared Pecans are tossed with a coating and spread on a cookie sheet to bake.

Cheese Pennies and Whiskey Balls can be stirred together in minutes. Sauce for the Open-Faced Shrimp Remoulade Sandwiches requires little more than mixing together a few condiments with chopped vegetables, and the shrimp take no time to boil (though you could spend extra on precooked ones).

Even the pork tenderloin is easy: It can be smoked on top of the stove while the ingredients for the blackberry ketchup simmer. As for the accompanying biscuits, they can be made and frozen a week early, then popped into the oven 30 minutes before guests arrive. The simplest hors d'oeuvre of all? A bottle of Pickapeppa sauce poured over cream cheese.

Pierrepont cut the bar bill by serving only bourbon—of course—but in three different drinks: Sazeracs, Whiskey Sours, and Bourbon-and-Branch Highballs. Most folks can handle just a few strong cocktails, so for 15 people, two or three fifths should cover you.

Like Natchez itself, Pierrepont's party was somewhat old-fashioned but also just debauched enough to give everyone a chance to "let the cat out" without "putting on airs," as the old-timers like to say. After all, they don't call Mississippi the Hospitality State for nothin'.

Open-Faced Shrimp Remoulade Sandwiches, opposite, were served Southern-style—on a silver tray. Above right: Friends made merry with bourbon-laced cocktails in hand.

A decanter of bourbon, left, was put to use spiking several cocktails, including this potent yet potable Sazerac. Above: Even Pierrepont (yes, one of *those* Pierreponts) knows you can get into the holiday spirit without spending a fortune on a fete. Opposite: Simple magnolia leaves and votive candles adorned the mantel.

1.   2.   3.   4.

Such a Card!

As Peggy Pierrepont's invite proves, simple handwritten notes can be a lot more charming—and cheaper—than printed ones. Ready to put pen to paper? Go on, skip the latest holiday selections: Customize old postcards you already have on hand. These are just a few springboards to get your creative juices flowing: 1. A Santa decal joins Elvis and Nixon in the Oval Office. 2. Glitter drifts hit the big city, topped by a tinsel knot. 3. A snippet of red ribbon lassos the legendary Jackalope. 4. Napoleon III considers who's been naughty and who's been nice.

Dressed-up guests cut loose in the down-home hospitality of Pierrepont's party. Opposite, from top to bottom: Sweet Chess Squares proved hard to resist; a classic Bourbon-and-Branch Highball filled a vintage glass advertising the 75-year-old *Delta Queen* steamboat, which still docks in Natchez; a bottle of Pickapeppa sauce was all it took to turn a block of cream cheese into a savory hors d'oeuvre.

THE RECIPES

cheese pennies
(makes about 100)

- 8 oz. sharp cheddar cheese, grated
- 1 stick (8 tbsp.) salted butter, cubed and softened
- 1 tsp. cayenne pepper
- 1 tsp. sugar
- ½ tsp. salt
- 1½ cups all-purpose flour

Preheat oven to 375°F. In a large bowl, combine cheese and butter. Stir in cayenne, sugar, and salt. Then stir in flour, ¾ cup at a time. Mix and knead thoroughly. (Or use a food processor to blend all ingredients except flour; add flour gradually and pulse until dough forms a ball.) Chill dough for 30 minutes, then form into marble-size balls and arrange on ungreased baking sheets. Flatten using a fork to make a crisscross pattern. Bake for 8 to 10 minutes and let cool. Store in airtight containers at room temperature.

spicy sugared pecans
(makes about 2 cups)

- 1 egg white, slightly beaten
- ¾ cup sugar
- 1 tsp. salt
- 1½ tsp. ground cinnamon
- ½ tsp. ground cloves
- ½ tsp. ground nutmeg
- 1 tsp. cayenne pepper
- 1 pat salted butter
- 2 cups pecan halves

Preheat oven to 300°F. In a large bowl, combine egg white with 1 tsp. water and beat lightly. Set aside. In a separate bowl, combine sugar, salt, and spices. Grease a baking sheet with butter. Using a slotted spoon, dip pecan halves in egg white mixture, allowing the excess liquid to drip back into the bowl. Then toss wet pecans in sugar mixture until well coated. Spread on a greased baking sheet. Bake for 35 minutes or until dry, turning at least once. Let cool completely, then store in airtight containers.

salt-roasted pecans
(makes about 2 cups)

- 1 stick (8 tbsp.) salted butter
- 2 cups pecan halves
  Salt, to taste

Preheat oven to 250°F. Melt butter in a saucepan. Add pecans and toss to coat. Spread in a single layer on an ungreased baking sheet. Bake for about 30 minutes or until pecans begin to darken. Drain on paper towels and sprinkle with salt. Let cool completely and store in airtight containers.

open-faced shrimp remoulade sandwiches
(makes 40)

- 1 tbsp. Old Bay seasoning
- 20 medium shrimp
- 1 loaf po'boy bread (or a skinny baguette), cut into 40 ¼-inch-thick slices
  Remoulade Sauce (see recipe, above right)
- 1 head iceberg lettuce, julienned
- 2 hard-boiled eggs, grated
  Pepper, to taste

Preheat oven to 250°F. In a stockpot, bring 6 cups water and Old Bay seasoning to a rolling boil. Peel, devein, and add shrimp; cook for 4 minutes or until pink. Drain and let cool. Place bread slices on ungreased baking sheets, toast for about 5 minutes, and set aside. Peel each shrimp and slice lengthwise. Toss all the shrimp with half of the remoulade. Spread ½ tsp. remaining sauce over each slice of bread. Then top with lettuce and a coated shrimp slice. Sprinkle with grated egg and pepper.

remoulade sauce
(makes 2½ cups, or enough for 40 sandwiches)

- 1 cup mayonnaise
- ½ cup chopped celery
- ½ cup chopped scallions
- ¼ cup chopped parsley
- ¼ cup prepared horseradish
- 1 lemon, juiced
- 2 tbsp. coarse mustard
- 1 tbsp. yellow mustard
- 2 tbsp. ketchup
- 2 tbsp. Worcestershire sauce
- 1 tbsp. white vinegar
- 1 tbsp. Louisiana Hot Sauce
- 1 tsp. minced garlic
- 2 tsp. paprika
  Salt, to taste

Place all ingredients in a large bowl and mix together thoroughly. Taste for seasoning and adjust.

biscuits with smoked pork tenderloin and blackberry ketchup
(makes 40)

- 2 7-inch (1 to 1¼ lb.) pork tenderloins
- 2 tbsp. olive oil
  Dash salt and pepper
  Carriage House Biscuits (see recipe on page 184)
  Blackberry Ketchup (see recipe on page 184)

Brush tenderloins with olive oil, sprinkle with salt and pepper, and smoke meat for about 20 to 25 minutes. (For directions, see caption on page 184.) To test for doneness, slice off a piece

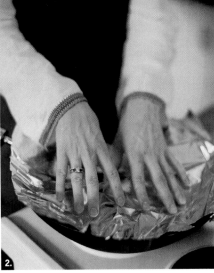

SMOKIN'

Don't have a giant smoker in your yard? Don't have a yard, period? No problem, says chef Courtney Taylor, above. You can still make smoked pork tenderloin with just a stove and a wok.

1. Soak a few handfuls of wood chips in water for 30 minutes, then throw them into an unheated wok (you can line your wok first with aluminum foil to keep the smoky residue from sticking).

2. Put another piece of foil over the wood chips and cover the wok with its lid. Heat on medium-high for 10 minutes.

3. Take the lid off and place the meat directly on the foil. Cover the wok and let the meat smoke for 20 to 25 minutes.

from one end and insert an instant-read thermometer. Medium-rare is 145°F, but if you prefer the meat well done, finish in a 350°F oven for 15 more minutes. Allow the meat to cool for 20 minutes, then slice thinly and set aside. Split each biscuit, spread 1 tsp. Blackberry Ketchup on the bottom half, and top with a layer of sliced pork.

carriage house biscuits
(makes 40)

- 2 cups all-purpose flour
- 4 tsp. baking powder
- ¼ tsp. salt
- 1 tsp. sugar
- 5 tbsp. vegetable shortening, chilled
- 1 cup cold milk

Preheat oven to 450°F. Mix all dry ingredients together in a large bowl, then cut in shortening. While stirring, add milk. Start with ¼ cup, add slowly, and stop when dough comes together. (Or mix dry ingredients together in a food processor. Then add shortening, pulsing until the mixture resembles coarse meal. With the machine running, pour milk through the feed tube until mixture forms a ball. Stop immediately.) Place dough on a lightly floured surface and roll to a thickness of about ¼ inch. Cut into 2-inch-wide biscuits. Gather up scraps, flatten, and cut more biscuits until all the dough has been used. Place on ungreased baking sheets and paint tops with remaining milk. Bake for 15 minutes or until golden. Split the tops and immediately butter them. (The formed, uncooked biscuits can be stored in the freezer for at least a week; do not thaw them before baking.)
Recipe courtesy of the

Carriage House Restaurant in Natchez.

blackberry ketchup
(makes 1½ cups, or enough for 40 sandwiches)

- 1 8-oz. jar seedless blackberry jam
- ½ cup white vinegar
- 2 tbsp. dark brown sugar
  Pinch ground ginger
- ½ tsp. ground cinnamon
- ¼ tsp. cayenne pepper
- ½ tsp. salt
- 1 tbsp. salted butter

In a small saucepan, heat blackberry jam with vinegar, sugar, and spices over medium-high heat. Allow mixture to come to a slow boil. Lower heat and simmer for 15 minutes. Add butter and stir until melted. Adjust seasoning to taste.

whiskey balls
(makes 36)

- 2½ cups vanilla wafers, finely crushed
- 2 tbsp. cocoa
- 3 cups confectioners' sugar

- 1 cup pecans, finely chopped
- 3 tbsp. white corn syrup
- ¼ cup bourbon

In a large bowl, combine crushed wafers, cocoa, 2 cups sugar, and nuts. In a separate bowl, mix corn syrup and bourbon; add to dry ingredients and mix well. Form into bite-size balls and roll them in remaining confectioners' sugar. Store in airtight containers until ready to serve.

chess squares
(makes 30 to 40)

- 1 18-oz. package yellow cake mix
- 3 eggs
- 1 stick (8 tbsp.) salted butter, melted
- 1 8-oz. package cream cheese
- 1 tsp. vanilla
- 1 1-lb. box confectioners' sugar, plus ½ cup for dusting

Preheat oven to 350°F. Combine cake mix, 1 egg,

Smoked pork tenderloin and blackberry ketchup update the classic Southern ham biscuit.

A vintage sectional dish separated the salty pecans from the sugary sweet ones. Opposite: Bourbon made yet another appearance—this time in Whiskey Balls rolled in confectioners' sugar.

THE RECEIPT

1 5-oz. bottle Pickapeppa sauce	$2.11
1 10.6-oz. box salted crackers	$1.92
8 oz. sharp cheddar cheese	$1.77
4 sticks salted butter	$1.79
1 2-lb. bag all-purpose flour	$1.29
6 eggs	$0.82
2 2-cup bags pecan halves	$7.64
1 box Old Bay seasoning	$2.99
20 medium shrimp	$3.64
1 loaf po'boy bread	$1.79
1 head iceberg lettuce	$0.98
1 bunch celery	$0.99
1 bunch scallions	$0.39
1 bunch parsley	$0.50
1 10-oz. jar prepared horseradish	$1.49
18 lemons	$3.06
1 9-oz. jar coarse mustard	$0.98
1 3-oz. bottle Louisiana Hot Sauce	$0.47
1 2.5-lb. package pork tenderloins	$8.15
1 12-oz. jar seedless blackberry jam	$1.56
1 1-lb. box dark brown sugar	$0.56
1 12-oz. bag vanilla wafers	$0.99
3 1-lb. boxes confectioners' sugar	$2.67
1 1-lb. bag chopped pecans	$3.28
2 1.75-1 bottles bourbon	$19.98
1 18-oz. box yellow cake mix	$0.75
2 8-oz. packages cream cheese	$1.76
1 750-ml bottle anise liqueur	$7.79
1 2-oz. set bitters	$3.29
6 oranges	$1.00
1 10-oz. jar maraschino cherries	$2.59
TOTAL (tax not included)	**$88.99**

ALREADY IN YOUR PANTRY: cayenne, sugar, salt, cinnamon, cloves, nutmeg, pepper, mayonnaise, yellow mustard, ketchup, Worcestershire, white vinegar, garlic, paprika, olive oil, baking powder, vegetable shortening, milk, ground ginger, cocoa, white corn syrup, vanilla

and melted butter in a large bowl. Stir until thoroughly blended. Spread batter in a greased 9-by-13-inch pan so it covers the bottom. Using an electric mixer, blend cream cheese, remaining eggs, vanilla, and confectioners' sugar. Pour this mixture on top of batter and bake for 35 minutes. Remove from the oven and slice into small squares, then return to the oven for 5 more minutes. Let cool, then take them out of the pan and dust them with ½ cup confectioners' sugar. Store in airtight containers at room temperature.

sazerac
(makes 1)

- ½ tsp. anise-flavored liqueur
- Cracked ice
- 1 tsp. confectioners' sugar
- ¼ tsp. bitters
- 1–2 oz. bourbon
- 1 strip lemon zest, for garnish

Pour liqueur into a chilled tumbler and swirl to coat. Fill a cocktail shaker with ice, then add sugar, bitters, and bourbon. Shake vigorously, then strain into the prepared tumbler. Garnish with lemon zest.

whiskey sour
(makes 1)

- ½ tsp. sugar (or 1 oz. simple syrup, above right)
- 1 oz. fresh lemon juice
- 2 oz. bourbon
- 1 orange slice
- 1 maraschino cherry

Put about 5 or 6 ice cubes in a cocktail shaker. Add sugar or syrup, lemon juice, and bourbon. Shake well and strain into a cocktail or sour glass. Garnish with orange slice and cherry.

simple syrup
(makes 2 cups)

- 1⅛ cups sugar

Bring sugar and 2¼ cups water to a boil, stirring until sugar dissolves. Reduce heat to low and simmer for 2 minutes. Remove from heat and let sit for 15 minutes. Syrup can be refrigerated in an airtight container for up to 2 weeks.

bourbon-and-branch highball
(makes 1)

- 2 oz. bourbon

Branch is an old term for a small, clear stream— in other words, a fancy, nostalgic way to say "water." Pour some, and a shot bourbon, into a highball glass filled with ice.

Resources

Even the most prolific hosts don't party all the time. Between budget bashes, each of the savvy social planners featured herein keeps busy with a paying gig. Here's how to find them:

January

I See London
  Jersey City, NJ
  www.iseelondon.net

Sue Keller's cotton lingerie line includes such under-garments as the coyly clever Bear Breasted Bra ($21), with two strategically placed animal patches, and the demure Picnic Boy Short ($12).

The Bubble Lounge
  New York, NY
  San Francisco, CA
  www.bubblelounge.com

At these bicoastal cham-pagne bars, co-owned by Eric Macaire (who provided our bubbly picks), you'll find sultry decor and more than 300 primo champagnes and sparkling wines.

February

Fabrica
  New York, NY
  212-587-6340
  fabricallc@hotmail.com
  for stores

Interior and textile designer Demi Adeniran brings her high-concept cloth creations to the masses with Fabrica, a line of bright, graphic duvets ($300 each) and matching pillowcases (three for $95).

April

Snow & Graham
  Chicago, IL
  www.snowand
  graham.com for stores

Stationery designer Ebony Snow Hurr creates hand-styled, vintage-inspired note cards and other paper designs out of her Ravenswood loft studio. Our favorite? The sassy "score" card, which depicts a bowling strike, for $3.

May

Jon Carloftis
  Erwinna, PA
  610-294-8057

Kentucky native Jon Carloftis has transformed outdoor spaces for the likes of Julianne Moore and Edward Norton. But you don't have to be a wealthy celeb to get a taste of the garden designer's style. Just stop by the Rockcastle River Trading Company (606-843-0854), the chic country store he operates (with his mother) in the Bluegrass State.

June

Love-Life
  Miami, FL
  www.lovelifeinc.com
  for stores

As its name suggests, Felice Pappas's clothing line is full of cheery, colorful dress designs (they appear throughout the pictures of her Latin luau). And the festive frocks start at just $100—you gotta love that.

July

Aqua Vitae Design
  Los Angeles, CA
  323-663-1777
  www.aquavitae
  design.com

Dynamic duo Alexandra and Eliot Angle own the interior design firm Aqua Vitae. For more hosting tips, see their snappy guide, *Cocktail Parties With a Twist* (Stewart, Tabori & Chang, $30), or catch their summer entertaining shows on the Fine Living Network.

AUGUST

Sparky's American Food
  Brooklyn, NY
  718-302-5151

Restaurateurs Brian Benavidez and Melissa Locker serve fresh, unfussy organic fare at Sparky's, their gourmet hot dog joint in Williamsburg, Brooklyn. Manhattanites will finally get to bite into a free-range Fearless Frank ($2.50) at a second Sparky's location set to open in late 2004.

September

Fuss
  Chicago, IL
  776-296-1015
  www.fusscustom.com

Graphic designer Jessica Murnane cofounded Fuss, Lincoln Park's hippest stationery boutique, in 2002. The emporium carries one-of-a-kind invitations, save-the-date cards, and thank-you notes ($2 to $6 each).

October

Children's book author William Joyce built up a devoted following with his best-selling *Rolie Polie Olie* (Laura Geringer Books, $16), which grew into an Emmy Award–winning Disney Channel program. Joyce is currently producing two animated films, one titled *Robots* and the other based on his quirky kid's tale *A Day With Wilbur Robinson* (HarperTrophy, $7).

November

Prune
  New York, NY
  212-677-6221

Chef Gabrielle Hamilton's tiny Lower East Side restau-rant, Prune, has won over both critics and casual diners in a big way by transforming humble supermarket staples into delicate gourmet cuisine. Prune's weekend brunch, in particular, attracts huge lines—which will give you time to choose among Hamilton's nine variations on the Bloody Mary.

DECEMBER

Former caterer Courtney Taylor cohosted and wrote about our Southern-inflected cocktail party. If you're still hungry for more down-home cooking ideas, check out Taylor's *The Southern Cook's Handbook* (Quail Ridge Press, $25) or her weekly food feature, which is syndicated in Gannett newspapers.

Photography Credits

Quentin Bacon
pages 5 (top middle), 78–83, 84 (top left and top right), 85–87, 89.

André Baranowski
pages 8, 10, 57, 61, 70 (top right).

John Dolan
pages 4 (bottom middle), 5 (top left), 9, 64, 66 (top left), 67–69, 70 (bottom right), 71–75, 119–127, 129.

R. Jerome Ferraro
pages 5 (bottom left), 144–153, 155 (top left), 156–157.

Ben Fink
pages 2, 14, 176–179, 180 (top left and top right), 181–187.

Jim Franco
page 13.

Steven Freeman
pages 12 (top left, middle left, and bottom left), 19, 33 (Nos. 2, 4, 5, 6, 8).

Christopher Gallo
pages 11 (bottom right), 128 (Nos. 2, 3).

Hugh Hartshorne
pages 4 (bottom right), 11 (top), 16, 132–141, 161, 166 (top left).

Rob Howard
pages 5 (top right), 92–103.

Deborah Jaffe
page 12 (bottom right).

Frances Janisch
and Chris Fanning
pages 4 (top middle), 38–47.

Eric Anthony Johnson
pages 37, 143.

Jon Lam/Detour Photo
pages 49, 63, 66 (bottom), 70 (top left), 77, 91, 105, 128 (Nos. 1, 4), 155 (top right), 159, 175.

Ericka McConnell
pages 4 (bottom left), 106–115.

Maura McEvoy
pages 4 (top right), 50–56, 58–59.

William Meppem
pages 5 (bottom middle), 160, 162–165, 166 (bottom right), 167–171, 173.

James Merrell
pages 4 (top left), 22–32, 34–35.

Julie Mihaly
pages 5 (bottom right), 180 (bottom).

Bradford Noble
page 17.

Melissa Punch
pages 21, 60, 84 (bottom right), 88, 117, 131, 154, 172.

Nathan Sayers
pages 7, 33 (Nos. 1, 3, 7).

Daniela Stallinger
page 18.

COVER
Hugh Hartshorne
back bottom.

James Merrell
back top.

Daniela Stallinger
front left and right.

LIGHTBULB ICON
Melissa Punch

Index